以資料為本的
校務決策績效評估

周景揚、王蒞君
主編

以資料為本的校務決策績效評估　序

臺灣校務研究專業協會（Taiwan Association for Institutional Research，簡稱TAIR）自2016年創立，並在黃榮村、廖慶榮兩位前任理事長帶領下逐漸蓬勃發展。除此之外，TAIR會務繁盛，除專業會員與大專院校會員數節節攀升，更藉著國際研討會打開新的視野、探究校務議題更深入之層面。

2019年末開始，我們迎來了巨大的挑戰與改變。新冠肺炎疫情擴散改變了傳統校園授課模式，進而擴及影響各校招生策略、課程規劃、國際生就學等各項事務。同時，我們進入必須隨時應疫情變化做出應變措施的快速決策時期。時間、空間壁壘正因為這波洶湧的全球疫情逐漸消解，高等教育的新路與探索就此開啟。

TAIR集結相關研究者，出版「以資料為本的校務決策績效評估」一書，集臺灣最新校務研究成果精華為一體，並以符合當代校務經營之趨勢變遷為背景，開展出一系列校務議題討論，內容多元遍及招生研究、國際化、職涯研究與學生就業探討……等一系列面向；此外，本書作者群來自公立、私立、一般與科技大學，他們的傾囊相授，以及寶貴的經驗分享，將帶領我們前往校務研究的里程碑。

隨著科技發展，高等教育肩負研究創新與作育英才之重責，日新月異的技術變化與時勢變遷，校務決策影響層面更勝以往。大學經營之於高等教育，是複雜且繁細的領域，除專業智識，管理透明、公開化外，校務研究近年立基於校務資料分析，逐漸朝著議題開發與國際鏈結的道路而去。「以資料為本的校務決策績效評估」一書，除象徵臺灣校務研究領域的推進，更也希望成為校務研究之活水，為校務決策提供有力之論證，達實用之效。

巨量資料雲集的時代，如何將資料整合成有益的資訊，並藉此輔助我們做出更加明確、理性的決策，將是最大的行動前提。數據為我們帶來更加理性的決策模式，也成為我們的指引——讓我們遠離過往決策中「跟著感覺走」的樣態；讓資訊、數據帶給我們更精確的選擇，避免產生無效的決策。而這除了與TAIR在新階段的重大使命「基於証據的大學校務決策思維」相符，同時亦是校務研究領域在未來的發展道路上，最重要的決策核心。

在改變之前，我們需要回歸最原始的本質思考。如此才不致迷失於眾多看似通往解法的捷徑裡，也將不再為了複雜的現況與無法預知的前景感到惶然。

最後，感謝「以資料為本的校務決策績效評估」一書中諸位作者的研究貢獻，為臺灣的高等教育、校務研究奠定邁向前路的基石！

臺灣校務研究專業協會第三屆理事長
周景揚

以資料為本的校務決策績效評估　序

距離疫情爆發的2019年末，已到了第四個年頭。新冠肺炎帶來的衝擊甚鉅，影響層面更是深遠。在這些日子裡，校務推展不停地因應著疫情狀況彈性變化。在仍有諸多變數的現在，疫情對於學術機構治理、教學成果的影響層次廣泛且難以避免，如何在後疫情時代下持續深化校務研究並開展其新的維度，更全面地在教學研究、校務治理上達輔助之效，是校務研究領域往後值得深入探索的一環，也是引人關注的趨勢。

在2020年，世界經濟論壇（The World Economic Forum，WEF）發布「未來學校」白皮書，其中「教育4.0」概念成為了未來高等教育的重要指引。此外，當今國內108課綱教育政策也即將迎來了第一屆新生，多元學習歷程成了評量的重要標準之一。各大高教機構在此背景下，如何因應大學招生，以及優化學校課程、評量模式，並延伸至學生畢業、就職等各面向議題，將會是校務研究全新的考驗。

「以資料為本的校務決策績效評估」一書以「教育4.0」作為開端，進而延伸至國際化、招生、學生職涯探討等諸多重要校務議題。在科技發展迅速的同時，「教育4.0」所強調的「創新產出」、「跨界連結」與「協同創造」，已成校務決策中需納入考量的重要前提。雖然，疫情因素讓許多國家不得不封鎖邊境，減少人員流動以遏止蔓延，但在無遠弗屆的網際網絡及國際化的趨勢下，仍可讓校務治理、教學研究成果展露於世界目光。各大機構所發布的「大學排名」，更是指引高等教育機構之各項指標，如：人力資源編制與國際合作等。同時，藉由大學排名結果揭示了現今高等教育機構已不再是歐美本位，亞洲許多高教機構整體排名逐漸上升；高教機構未來所需面對的挑戰，除國際目光省視與國家政策推行之外，如何藉由巨量數據調整策略，穩固亞洲高等教育之地位，也將是我們在校務研究領域中值得關注的議題。

校務研究核心在於「如何使教育機構評估推動成效」，除卻校務治理，學生作為教育機構中最重要的核心角色，亦是研究重點之一。從招生開始，如何利用尺規精準招生，並讓學生在教育過程中獲得更多元、豐富的探索，更讓學生在學以致用之餘，至畢業後就業，將所學與就業趨勢結合。除卻我們所熟知的「硬技能」、「軟實力」，如何藉學習過程中探索可能，開展不同領域間的跨度融合，這在在都是教育機構所積極發展並深切盼望的狀態。

「以資料為本的校務決策績效評估」中，更是以高等教育機構方與進入職場後的學生角度，以雙邊資訊分別展示了職能、職涯領域將如何走向雙贏的道路。同時，藉由大量數據分析，也將輔助教育機構在往後的職能推廣、學生職涯發展計畫等決策上有著更多的依據，更加完善決策前整體之調查與評估，讓決策真正發揮用處。

感謝TAIR協會，亦感謝「以資料為本的校務決策績效評估」一書；近年來，台灣校務研究的推行能有如此成效，並讓Evidence-based的決策模式在高教界被廣泛接受，TAIR及在校務研究領域默默耕耘的研究者們皆是最大功臣！同時，我們也希望能在往後看見校務研究越發蓬勃茁壯！

國立陽明交通大學校長
林奇宏

目次

從教育4.0看校務研究之未來發展與實踐

國立陽明交通大學校務大數據研究中心助理研究員
魏彗娟、羅孟婷

國立陽明交通大學電機工程學系講座教授
王蒞君

壹、前言

隨著全球化與資訊科技快速發展，「工業4.0」（Industry 4.0）的浪潮也席捲而來，許多產業發展、生活形式、教育模式以及學習型態，都隨著第四次工業革命產生極大的轉變與衝擊。所謂工業4.0，強調以「智慧製造」為革命重點，利用物聯網（Internet of Thing，簡稱IoT）、雲端運算（Cloud computing）、人工智慧（Artificial Intelligence，簡稱AI）與機器學習（Machine learning）等技術，提高自動化程度並採用智慧型工廠，運用資料分析以更高效率和生產力來製造商品，將傳統生產方式轉為高度客製化、智慧化、服務化的商業模式（Frank et al., 2019）。整體而言，工業4.0是連結虛擬與現實的橋樑，讓製造過程高度智慧化，逐漸成為製造主流（IBM, n.d.; Lee et al., 2015）。

長期以來，教育的規劃與發展受到社會變遷、經濟成長和科技進展的影響，而改變教育的目標、策略與作為。就整個教育發展的歷史而言，其過程與工業革命具有密不可分的關係（Kazimirov, 2018）。大學生如何從學校所提供的課程與活動，學習及培養未來職涯發展的關鍵能力，以及如何面對工業4.0所帶來的挑戰及人才需求，成為高等教育關注的議題（Demartini & Benussi, 2017）。事實上，面對科技產業與資訊社會的變革，許多國家已經開始提出因應工業4.0關於經濟發展與人才培育的相關政策，期望透過創新科技與思維模式培養符合未來社會需求的人才，進而帶動全球經濟社會的發展。對此，在工業4.0的推動下，新型態的教育系統與模式也開始進行轉型——「教育4.0」（Education 4.0）也隨之而生（e.g. Iyer, 2018; Kunnari et al., 2019; Schwab, 2016）。

美國未來學家、明尼蘇達大學副教授Harkins（2008）認為「二十一世紀，第一個躍升到教育4.0階段的國家，將成為人力發展的領頭羊，並創造二十一世紀新經濟。」Harkins更指出，教育4.0是以「創新產出」為核心的教育，強調培養學習者具備跨界連結、協同創造的能力。德國僱主協會主席Kramer（2017）也提出，若要迎接工業4.0的挑戰，需要提供學生最符合未來社會需求的學習環境，而教育就是一個最佳的途徑。根據2020年世界經濟論壇（The World Economic Forum，簡稱WEF）所發布的「未來學校」報告（The World Economic Forum, 2020），因應工業4.0，全球進入「教育4.0」的時代，教育將更具科技化、智慧化和數位化，強調自主學習，讓學生可以根據自身的學習進度與成效進行自我調整，並透過資訊科技的輔助，隨時檢視與診斷自己的學習情形，讓學習更加個人化。因應「工業4.0」而推動的「教育4.0」，為學校教育帶來需要面臨的挑戰，由於學校扮演著「培育人才」的關鍵角色，要如何應對教育4.0所帶來的教育改變，發展變革創新教育模式的首要場域，變得極為重要。

2019年COVID-19疫情爆發更顛覆了世界各地的教育系統。過去教師與學生習慣於到實體教室面對面上課，但因為疫情的關係，學校必須轉換成利用各種視訊會議軟體（如Google Meet、ZOOM、Webex等）進行線上課程，這對學校、教師、學生甚至家長都是一大考驗，若無法順利轉換並適應新的學習型態，有可能造成學習的大斷層（Sarma & Yoquinto, 2021）。如所見，在2019與2020年，無論是哪一個國家，皆顯露了教育系統在因應重大改變或制度時無法快速因應，顯示其韌性（Resilience）不足之處。同樣地，未來全球化與數位化會更加顯著，許多工作強調數位能力、社交情感技能、創新思考、甚至團隊凝聚力、溝通互動等關鍵能力，若教育系統所培養的人才無法滿足未來社會需求，那麼極有可能對生產力和社會凝聚力帶來更多風險。整體而言，面對全球經濟與資訊科技的快速發展，傳統教育制度與學習內容可能不足以因應現今社會的需求，我們應該將學習的主動權回歸學生，強調以學習者為中心的學習型態，應用創新科技及創新思維，以多元創新的教學模式進行教學，培養學生具備包容性、凝聚力及生產力的關鍵技能，以因應未來社會的人才需求與產業發展趨勢。

大學作為國家產業人才培育的主要機構，如何因應教育4.0對教育制度與教學型態所帶來的轉變與影響，在兼顧校務發展與產業需求的情況下，針對教育制度提出改革創新，培養具備二十一世紀關鍵能力的重要人才，成為每一所大學的首要任務。舉例來說，當學校改變修課制度，給學生更大的彈性去自由選擇不同領域的課程，參與更多課外活動，期望學生能培養第二或第三專長，進行跨領域的學習。若學校想要知道其推動成效，瞭解學生是否真的因為彈性修課制度有更多跨領域學習的機會，就需要進行相關的校務研究分析，透過有計畫、系統地蒐集資料、分析評估與結果闡釋，提供學校決策時的參考。因此，我們可以知道，大學在面臨教育4.0所帶來的衝擊，需要作出許多調整與創新，透過校務研究不僅能讓學校在進行相關教育制度的創新時確實掌握校務發展方向，以因應未來產業發展趨勢，也能夠透過數據分析結果瞭解學校人才培育的成效，同時提升辦學績效及學校競爭力。

貳、教育4.0之意涵

何謂「教育4.0」（Education 4.0）？Harkins（2008）指出，教育4.0是以創新產出為核心的教育，強調跨界連結、協同創造。Kunnari等人（2019）認為教育4.0讓教學與學習產生改變，資訊科技與網際網路所帶來的數位化學習，讓學習不受時間與空間的限制；教學不再以教師為中心，而改以學習者為中心，教師的角色也轉變成學習的促進者（facilitators），學習開始著重多方面的關鍵能力培養。根據Sinlarat（2016）的說法，教育4.0是一個全新的學習系統，針對教與學提出一個創新的概念，學生在整個學習過程中利用新興科技與技術發展終身學習和專業知能，以適應未來社會的需求。同樣地，Hussin（2018）也指出教育4.0主要目的在於學習者能夠利用資訊科技與網際網路所提供的平台或載具，實現不受時間與地點限制的自主學習，讓學習過程變得更加快捷、便利且有效率。換言之，教育4.0讓學習者能夠有更多的學習自主權，可以依據自己的需求與能力自我決定如何學習以及何時學習（Deaconu et al., 2018）。統整過去文獻，我們可以知道，教育4.0指的不是創新技術，而是希望在教育系統與制度上做創新的改變，其主要目標是讓學生能夠將所學知識做更好的連結與統整，學習上不再只是傳統學科知識的理解與背誦記憶，更強調的是跨學科知識整合的能力，如何利用所學知識及能力透過新興資訊科技解決生活或工作層面可能面臨的問題或挑戰，如同教育部十二年國民基本教育課程綱要（教育部，2014）所強調的以「核心素養」為主軸，培養孩子成為「終身學習者」之目標，認為身處資訊和知識爆炸的數位時代，我們的現代教育必須有所轉變，除了教授學科知識，培養孩子擁有面對挑戰、解決問題的能力更顯重要，強調教育必須達到知識、能力與態度三面向，才能具備適應現在生活及面對未來挑戰的能力，而這項目標也與教育4.0的精神不謀而合。

整體而言，教育4.0的目的是將學生培養成擁有自學能力的成人，我們需要重新思考教育應該如何滿足全球不斷變化的人才需求，讓更多學習者能夠適應變化，並更有意義的建設自己的未來（Bujang et al., 2020）。如此的理念也將考驗教學現場教師的教學能力與整合能力，未來教學內容不只是素養導向還要跨領域結合，這些都是未來教師所要面臨的挑戰，顯現出教學的困境。

一、大學教育面臨教育4.0可能的挑戰

大學教育是未來產業人才培育的一環，為工業4.0時代的產業培育重要且需要的人才。而因應教育4.0帶來的挑戰與改變，大學教育所扮演的角色更是關鍵（Salmon, 2019; Xing, 2019）。2019年，英國聯合資訊系統委員會（The Joint Information Systems Committee，簡稱JISC）發布一份報告書（2019 JISC Horizon Report）（JISC, 2019），羅列了大學面臨教育4.0可能遇到的問題或挑戰。由表1所示，無論是在教學研究、學生學習、校務發展以及資安保護等議題都可能因為新興資訊科技或創新應用服務的發展而受到一定程度的影響，甚至在教育4.0的推動下，許多制度或模式也需要隨之改變。

表1　教育4.0面臨的挑戰與新興科技應用

挑戰	新興科技
Education and research finance	AI, IoT, Immersive technologies
Marketisation of education	Blockchain
Student experience	AI, Chatbots, Learning analytics

挑戰	新興科技
Skill gap	Immersive technologies, Simulations, AI
Bricks and clicks	Big Data, Robotics, Smart Library Management
Innovations in teaching and learning	AI, Personalized learning environment, Chatbots, Immersive technologies
Metrics and rankings	Data analytics
Attracting and retaining	AI, Immersive technologies
Open science and research infrastructure	AI, Robotics, Machine learning, Automated experimentation, Knowledge discovery tools, Connected research equipment
Cyber security	IoT （Security risks）

引自JISC (2019)，p.226。

舉例來說，在人工智慧（AI）、大數據分析（Big Data）等技術尚未成熟的時候，若要瞭解每位教師的教研表現，需以表單填寫的方式做大規模調查，資料整理歸納之後進行統計分析，不僅步驟程序繁雜，也需要花費許多人力進行相關作業。但當AI與大數據分析的概念與技術發展成熟，透過大數據資料庫建置，連結論文或教學系統，即可將資料詳實紀錄，像是Elsevier的SciVal科研分析管理工具[1]，以文獻與引用資料庫Scopus為資料來源，透過內建模組平台，校務研究人員可快速掌握教師與研究人員的學術表現，不僅能瞭解學校的優劣勢，也能客觀地找到學校於全球高等教育機構中的定位，制定新的策略以及找到新的標竿學校，發掘新的合作夥伴，協助學校掌握競爭優勢。又例如，過去想瞭解學生的學習行為表現，多以班級課程為單位進行量化或質化的教育研究，獲得的結果經常受限於資料量過少無法推論更多的學生族群或做出趨勢預測。但當學習分析、演算法、個人學習輔助應用等技術逐漸成熟，利用相關學習輔助工具如聊天機器人（Hien et al., 2018; Villegas-Ch et al., 2020）或智慧型手機應用程式進行學習活動，隨時記錄學生的學習

[1] SciVal科研分析管理工具（https://www.scival.com/landing）

行為，並且利用AI與大數據分析，即時分析學生的學習狀況，提供學生自我檢視學習進度，同時也可同步提供教師瞭解並掌握每位學生的學習動態，形成具數位化與智慧化的學習模式。而上述這些例子，都是因為新興科技技術的發展，帶動教育模式的改變，進而改變學生學習型態以及教師扮演的角色，這些都將是面臨教育4.0時我們需要共同面對的挑戰。

二、大學教育面臨教育4.0的人才培育

面對高度科技化與智慧化的社會，身為教育4.0的新世代，除了習得科技能力之外，成為具有人文素養和人性關懷的現代化公民，迎合產業發展的需求具備重要的關鍵能力，培養學生成為能夠符合未來產業或社會發展需求的人才，是大學教育須面對的重要議題。根據2020年世界經濟論壇WEF所發布的「未來學校」報告（The World Economic Forum, 2020），提出一個以教育4.0為基礎，符合未來經濟社會需求的一種新型態教育框架（見圖1）。此教育框架以學習內容及學習經驗二大重點，羅列八個關鍵要素，包括全球公民能力（Global citizenship skills）、創新和創造力（Innovation and creativity skills）、科技能力（Technology skills）、人際交往能力（Interpersonal skills）、個人化和自定進度學習（Personalized and self-paced learning）、可及性和包容性學習（Accessible and inclusive learning）、問題導向與協作學習（Problem-based and collaborative learning）、終身學習和以學生為中心的學習（Lifelong and student-driven learning）等。前四項主要是技能適應的內在機制，是現代公民必須具備的四項能力；後四項則是技能適應的方法機制，是反應未來工作與學習型態的創新模式。

Figure 2: The World Economic Forum Education 4.0 Framework

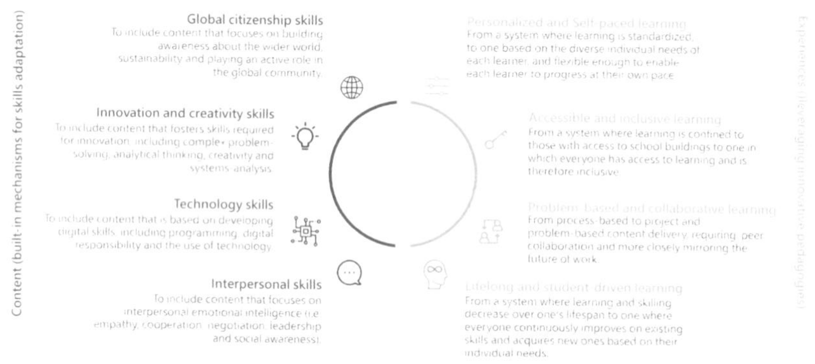

圖1　教育4.0的新型態教育框架

引自 The World Economic Forum (2020)，p.7。

三、教育4.0的新型態教育框架

當全世界都開始邁向教育4.0時，符合未來社會經濟生產的需求的人才應該具備什麼樣的能力，成為教育領域探討的重要議題。哈佛商學院教授巴登（Leonard-Barton, 1998）首先提出「T型能力」（T-Shaped Skills）之概念（如圖2），認為兼具專業與跨領域知識的T型通才比起傳統教育培養的對單一知識專精深耕的I型專業人才更加符合產業所需。所謂T型人才，指的是在英文字母「T」中，縱向的「I」代表知識的深度，指除了有廣博的知識外中，更對其中一個領域更有專業能力，亦稱為「硬實力」；橫向的「一」代表知識的廣度，指的是能與其他領域的專家跨學科合作，並將知識應用於非主要領域的廣度或能力，也稱之為「軟實力」。

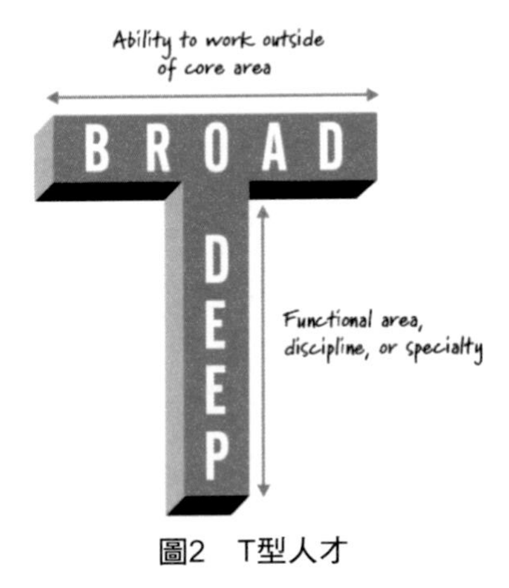

圖2　T型人才

引自 Kenneth (2012)，p.202

荷蘭教育委員會引用Leonard-Barton（1998）的「T型能力」之概念，定義出七種未來人才需要的「橫向能力」（transversal competence）（OECD, 2017），包含1、思考與學習的能力；2、文化識讀、互動與表述能力；3、自我照顧、日常生活技能與保護自身安全的能力；4、多元識讀（multi-literacy）；5、數位能力；6、工作生活能力與創業精神；7、參與、影響，並為可持續的未來負責等（洪詠善，2016）。伊拉斯莫斯大學教授凡德威爾德（Walter Vandervelde）針對「T型人才」做了一份研究，最後總結出了五大核心技能：創意（Creativity）、批判性思考（Critical Thinking）、自我管理（Self-management）、社交智慧（Social Intelligence）、注意力管理（Attention Management），並指出未來工作技能的要求都離不開這五大基本能力，但是這不代表只要各別精通這五種能力即可成為「T型人才」，重點是要學會如何組合運用這些能力（Vandervelde, 2021）。T型人才強調的就是靈活性和創造性。世界經濟論壇WEF報告指出，預計在2025年機器人或機器可取代人類超過一半的工作（The World Economic Forum, 2020）。相比只有單一的知識，T型人才除了擁有各種通用才能，在專業知識上也具有較深的理解能力和獨到見解，工作時能夠能將這些技能交叉運用，不單是機器無法取代，其獨特性更是他人無法取代。對於公司而言，培養「T型技能」能提升團隊成員之間（或團隊之間）的溝通與合作效率，從而提升公司整體的工作效率。對於個人而言，「T型人才」的核心概念在於終身學習，意即隨時保持對新事物的好奇心與求知欲，並且不斷學習新知、習得新技能。

而在教育4.0與產業發展的帶動下，對於人才的能力需求更加多樣化，甚至是希望每個人除了自身專業之外，還能夠擁有更多專業技能，並進行跨領域學習與合作，根據IBM《2012全球CEO調查報告》（IBM, 2021），結果指出市場對於人才的需求正在改變，從前需要的是具備單一技能的專業者，現在則需要專業多工的「π型人」。所謂「π型人才」，指的是除了對自身專業技能有高掌握度之外，同時擁有兩種以上專業技能，且具備跨領域的觀察角度與歷練的人，能對事件進行全面性的剖析與理解，創造出更高的價值。換言之，π型人才具備了複合性、發展性、創新性及競爭性等多種特質，除了擁有雙專長、熟悉雙領域、懷有雙視野外，更具備跨專長、跨領域、跨視野的能力，是未來產業及社會發展重要的複合型人才。對於大學教育來說，如何培育具韌性且專業的跨域人才、鼓勵跨領域學習，甚至擁有多種專業技能，成為能夠面對外界變化的π型人才，儼然成為大學教育不可忽視的議題。根據經濟合作暨發展組織（Organization for Economic Cooperation and Development，簡稱OECD）的報告《Future of Education and Skills 2030》（OECD, 2018），指出2030年每個人應該具備的核心能力應涵蓋知識（Knowledge）、技能（Skills）、特質與態度（Attitudes and Values）以及後設學習（Meta-cognitive skills）等面向（如圖3）。知識方面以跨學科為主，並將傳統與現代知識做整合，以主題或議題的方式

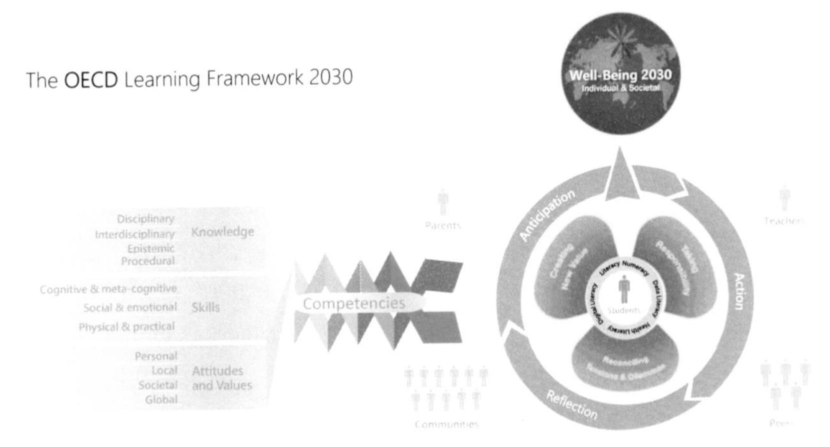

圖3　OECD 2030學習框架

引自OECD (2018)。

進行理解與掌握；技能則是需要培養創造力、批判思考、溝通能力及協同合作的能力；特質與態度包括警覺心、好奇心、勇氣、彈性或復原力、倫理及領導力等；而最重要的是後設學習，學習如何學習，懂得對自己的學習過程進行反思，檢視自己如何學習以及學到了什麼，讓自己更瞭解自己的學習。

在台灣，教育部也因應教育4.0，積極推動「以學習者為中心」之教育方式，培養學生具備二十一世紀關鍵核心能力（5C），包括：溝通協調能力（Communication）、團隊合作能力（Collaboration）、複雜問題解決能力（Complex problem solving）、批判思考能力（Critical thinking）、創造力（Creativity）。教育部於2014年推動「新一代數位學習計畫」，致力於提升學生的閱讀與5C能力，並希望透過多元彈性的磨課師課程（MOOC），提供以學習者為中心的個人化教育，發展教師創新教學，進而提高學生的學習成效。在大學方面，以國立台灣大學（以下簡稱台大）為例，為了能夠培養每一位畢業生具備更完善的關鍵能力，台大不僅提供輔導資源，鼓勵學生從參與式學習、社團活動中建置個人的人際關係網絡，更於2020年推動各系訂立「領域專長」[2]，每個領域有3至4門核心課程，方便學生擬定自己的跨域專長地圖。為了因應教育4.0所帶來的教育型態改變，讓學生的學習型態多樣化，台大也設立了多間高度科技化的「未來教室」[3]，讓學生可以一面看教室前方的課程簡報，一面用座位旁的電子白板討論，從牆面到桌面都能書寫，更有利於翻轉教學。另外如國立成功大學教務長王育民教授所言：「成大不只想培育企業最愛的好員工，更想養成改變社會與世界的領導人才」，因此，成大積極推動「第十學院CollegeX」跨域實踐平台[4]，以彈性化開課制度，回應提升學習動機誘因，套入基石課程與統整課程於多元學習模式，對接聯合國永續發展目標的議題導向學習，進行跨領域及實踐的教與學。目的是讓老師社群與學生群體可以透過教學與研究，定義未來的新問題，開展適當的解法，並自真正的冒險落實。CollegeX是未來能力與素養的養成的場域，跨域教學及實踐的創新場域，也是成功大學想像未來大學樣貌的實驗場域。同樣地，在2021年2月合併的國立陽明交通大學，也針對學生關鍵能力培養做出了許多教育制度的變革與策略，例如跨域學程、醫學系的醫師科學家組與醫生工程師組、百川學士學位學程、創創工坊等，其目的皆是希望能夠學校提供多樣化的學習方式，鼓勵學生跨領域學習、拓展個人人際網絡、培養多面向的專長，甚至是問題解決能力、協同合作等關鍵能力，以作為未來企業與社會所需的專業人才。以跨域學程來說，是以畢業學分不增加（或僅有少

---

[2] 國立臺灣大學領域專長實施要點https://www.dlc.ntu.edu.tw/%e6%95%99%e5%ad%b8%e6%96%b0%e7%9f%a5-%e9%a0%98%e5%9f%9f%e5%b0%88%e9%95%b7%e6%a8%a1%e7%b5%84-2/

[3] 臺大未來教室https://www.dlc.ntu.edu.tw/%E6%9C%AA%E4%BE%86%E6%95%99%E5%AE%A4/

[4] 成功大學第十學院CollegeX https://collegex.ncku.edu.tw/

量增加）的前提下進行，透過彈性學分的設計，搭配系所核心課程的模組化，並以生活學習社群及彈學導師制度為後援，提供學生更大的彈性學習空間，培育具國際移動力的跨領域人才。

由上述可看出，大學教育是培育國家人才的重要機構，對於如何培養學生具備關鍵核心能力以成為未來職場上所需要的專業人才，從教育階段順利轉銜進入職涯階段，是大學教育必須的義務也是挑戰。而我們也看到各大學在教育4.0的帶動下，紛紛針對學生特質以及學校特色推動一系列教育制度改革，包括多樣化的教學模式、彈性自主的修課制度、多元招生方式等。面對這些制度上的改變與創新，大學要如何評估推動成效也成為一項重要任務。

大學教育不同於中小學教育，因治校自主權擴增、大學教育市場化與國際化等因素，大學自身必須針對學校財政、招生競爭、教學品質及辦校績效責任等面向進行多方面評估與檢討，就如同企業一般進行有效地管理，以確保學校的校務治理績效以及辦學目標是有效且正確的。在大學推動各項教育變革以因應教育4.0所帶來的教學型態與學習模式改變以及未來產業和社會發展需求的過程中，應更加重視該如何運用校務研究於大學學生管理、各項資料蒐集分析以確保校務治理效能，強調大學治理的客觀性，以證據為本形成決策模式。校務研究對於大學校務治理來說扮演極為重要的角色，透過盤點、整合、管理及應用校內外既有的資料庫、資訊系統數據，建構一個可以長期追蹤學校辦學成效、學生學習歷程的資料平台，並利用縝密的校務資料分析和規劃策略方案，掌握學校發展脈動和國內外高等教育改革趨勢，建立學校行政與教學單位數據本位、績效責任的決策支持模式（王蒞君、劉奕蘭，2020；彭森明，2019）。

參、教育4.0下的校務研究

國立陽明交通大學（以下簡稱本校）於2015年成立「大數據研究中心」，並在2021年2月1日合校後，改名為「校務大數據研究中心」（以下簡稱本中心）。本中心結合資訊技術和校務研究，針對學生學習成效評估以及校務發展績效提供以證據為本的分析報告，協助學校領導、行政及教學單位做為決策之參考。為提出本校中長程校務發展白皮書，在林奇宏校長的帶領下，廣納校內師生的意見，透過共識凝聚，形成具十年願景的三年校務發展方向，提出「一樹百穫」計畫[5]。本中心也於行動綱領之「善用大數據 落實校務研究」章節中，針對校務研究提出三年計畫十年願景（如圖4所示），期以數據為主、人為本，透過資料蒐集分析與加值利用，以學生為中心進行校務議題評估，掌握國際高等教育改變之脈動與產業趨勢，提供實證數據建構校務大數據數位治理決策環境，協助本校發揮永續、創新、包容的精神，持續為產、官、學、研培育具有影響力與貢獻性之關鍵人才。

如圖4所示，因應本校的校務推動與發展，本中心以三大面向作為首要工作任務，包括：建置校務大數據數位治理決策環境、學術聲譽趨勢分析、發展校務研究議題分析。

一、建置校務大數據數位治理決策環境

發展校務資料管理系統，建立校務大數據數位治理決策環境，以證據／數據為本協助本校制定決策、落實行政效能、提升教學品質。

[5] 國立陽明交通大學「一樹百穫計畫」https://nycu-plan.tw/

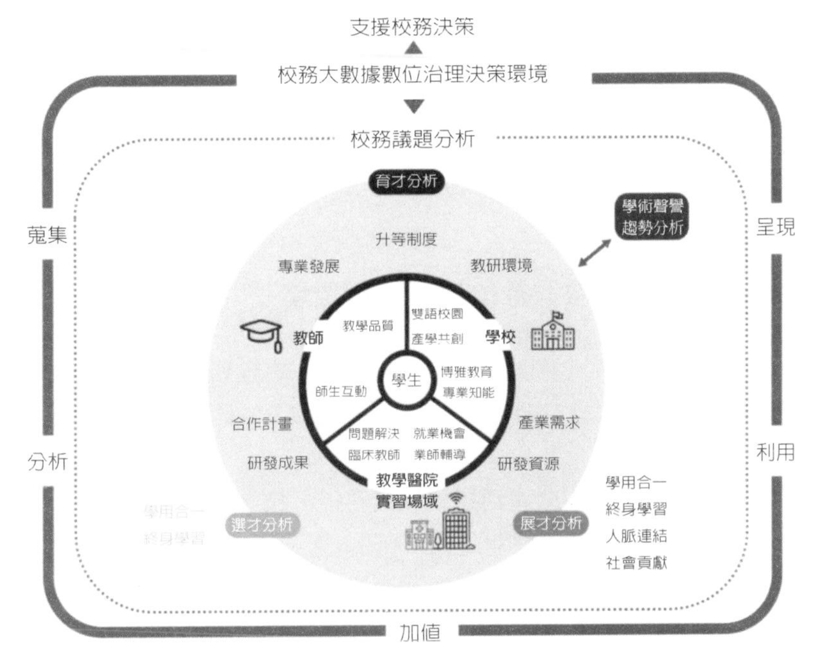

圖4　校務大數據研究中心中長程計劃之具體策略架構

1. 廣納異質校務資料，完善數位資料治理模式，強化自動化資料處理與資料分析流程，推動校務資料循環再生與利用，提高資訊品質與行政效率。
2. 資料加值運用，提高校務資料之透明性，例如動態資訊儀表板、校庫資料填報公開資訊。
3. 持續發展校務資料倉儲，強化校務資料收集整合與循環再生利用，支持各類議題發展與決策等應用。

二、學術聲譽趨勢分析

1. 分析本校世界大學學術排名、國內外企業對本校畢業生評價調查、及國內外高教趨勢，給予校方關於校務、學務、及教務等策略制定之回饋與參考。

2. 彙整本校各單位與永續發展相關質量化資料、定期維護永續發展成果網站與出版永續發展年報以作為和利害關係人之溝通平台與工具，強化本校與國際之連結性及影響力。

三、建置校務大數據數位治理決策環境

應用校務資料，發展選才、育才、展才之校務研究議題分析，支持本校培育能與社會及產業結合並接軌國際的跨領域人才之政策擬定及推動。

1. **選才分析**——以達到招生品質管控、精準招生為目的：

（1）建置學習歷程長期分析系統。

（2）提供實證資料協助招生評量尺規與選才標準校正。例如：定期進行入學書審與面試審查信度和學生就學後表現分析、各高中學生學習歷程與就學表現建模。

2. **育才分析**——以學生為中心，針對教師、學校、教學醫院／實習場域三方面進行校務議題評估，提供分析結果給予本校主責單位參考：

（1）教師：教研環境、升等制度、專業發展。

（2）學校：學生關鍵能力培養、師生互動與課程參與、產學共創學程新制、跨域融合、雙語校園國際接軌、博雅教育等。

（3）教學醫院／實習場域：問題解決能力、未來就業機會、學生對訓練場域之滿意度、臨床教師／業師與學生之間的關係或輔導方法等。

3. **展才分析**——連結畢業生、學校、雇主三方資料進行分析，提供結果給予本校主責單位參考：

（1）評估畢業生職涯規劃及個人專業成長的情形，並瞭解就業力與職場表現與企業需求之一致性。

（2）評估畢業生就業狀況，協助本校強化與產業之鏈結。

以下將針對本中心提出之三大策略中—學術聲譽趨勢分析、建置校務大數據數位治理決策環境之三個面向「選才、育才、展才」，分享在面對教育4.0，本中心在校務研究實踐與執行的重要研究案例予以讀者參考。

肆、教育4.0下的校務研究實踐與案例分享

一、選才分析

我國教育部於103年開始推動十二年國民基本教育，提出「十二年國民基本教育課程綱要總綱」，並於108年正式上路，因此又稱「108課綱」。此課綱以「適性揚才、終身學習」為願景，重視彈性與自主學習，尊重個別差異，希望孩子能夠作為學習的主人，具有學習的動機與熱情、有與人和社會互動的能力、並能將課程中學到的知識、技能與生活經驗連結，願意致力於社會、自然與文化的永續發展，成為具有社會適應與應變力的終身學習者（教育部，2014）。因應108課綱，高中課程規劃與大學升學制度都有大幅改變，為了讓大專院校選才與高中育才在此變革下能緊密銜接，教育部於106學年度試辦、108學年度落實各大專院校「大學招生專業化發展」及108學年度推動「建置高中學習歷程檔案」。大專院校透過「大學招生專業化發展」強化個人資料審查專業性，建置申請入學審查時的評量尺規（Rubric），培訓校內專業審查者，以篩選出適才適所，適合各校系所需的人才（教育部高教司，2018；教育部大學招生委員會聯合會，2019）。

綜觀台灣大專院校招生政策發展歷程[6]，從91學年度推動的「大學多元入學方案」讓招生管道多元化、93學年度將招生管道簡化為考試分發與甄選入學（包含個人申請與學校推薦）兩個管道、96學年度推動「大學繁星計畫」以實現高中均質、區域均衡理念，及100學年度大學繁星計畫與學校推薦整併為「大學繁星推薦」。這將近10年的招生政策變革，造就了目前大專院校有主要三大招生／入學管道：個人申請、繁星推薦、分發入學。「大學多元入學方案」目的為讓學生能選擇適合的升學管道，展現個人特質與潛力。然而，此三大入學管道仍較適用於目前在主流教育體制下升學的學生。為了讓招生管道更具包容性，使具有特殊才能與不同教育背景的學生（如境外臺生、新住民、弱勢族群、實驗教育學生等）也能與主流教育體制下的學生享有同樣的教育權利，教育部104學年度推動「大學辦理特殊選才招生試辦計畫」，107學年度「特殊選才招生」成為正式入學管道之一。108課綱正式上路後，高中課程轉以核心素養導向，鼓勵學生自主學習，111年考招新制即將上路，指定科目考試將改為分科測驗，以「個人申請」為主要招生管道，除學科能力測驗成績外，更加重視在校修課歷程與多元表現。

在多年招生政策的變革下，本校除了主要的三大招生／入學管道外，目前也在某些領域或學程設有特殊選才招生方式，如交大校區的百川學士學位學程、資訊工程學系、電機工程學系，及陽明校區生物醫學影像暨放射科學系等。為因應考招變化，如何有效協助各學系與學程進行精準招生成為各大專院校客不容緩的議題。為達到招生品質管控、精準招生之目的，本校建置「學習歷程長期分析系統」，提供實證資料協助招生評量尺規與選才標準校正，讓招生專業審查委員得以使用數據證據與各學系多年招生經驗傳承，找到

---

[6] 以下資料從中華民國教育部部史全球資訊網整理（https://history.moe.gov.tw/policy.asp?id=3）

興趣、志向、能力與校系相符人才（鄭朝陽、林珊如，2020）。例如：定期進行入學書審與面試審查信度和學生就學後表現分析、各高中學生學習歷程與就學表現建模。此外，為了校內招生專業人員可以即時取得與招生相關之校務分析資料，協助業務執行與佐證決策，本校建置校務數據視覺化平台，其主題涵蓋面向包含：招生入學資訊、歷年大學部各科系多元入學管道生源分析與入學後學習表現、就學穩定率追蹤、歷年生師比動態追蹤、模擬書審評委評分一致性、國際處歷年外籍學生比例變化等。本校個人申請入學管道，採計的項目除大學入學考試中心辦理之學科能力測驗外，也涵蓋書面審查及面談表現，其中每位學生的書面審查資料及面談表現兩個項目皆由多位專業招生審查與面試委員進行。除了訂定精準、公平、明確的評量尺規外，因審查過程多少含有主觀判斷的成分，為確保多位審查委員給予學生的分數達到一定的一致性與穩定性，對於評審結果有一定程度的共識，需仰賴審查委員間對評量尺規的一致了解與審查前的溝通與訓練。此外，也可經由校務研究每年分析每位審查委員給予的評分分數一致性信度與穩定性。本中心在選才分析之校務研究議題中，已經協助本校在精準招生方面進行相關研究分析：

（一）招生評量尺規檢驗

本中心每年協助各系所檢視審查委員間評分分數一致性信度，像是目前已協助至少兩個學系進行個人申請書面審查資料及面談表現的評分者信度檢驗，同時，也邀請審查委員定期進行模擬書面審查訓練，期許經由不斷的訓練與溝通，檢視評量尺規的適切性及審查委員對於尺規的一致性了解，並持續以統計數據檢評估審查委員對於分數的共識程度是否達到可接受的標準，也針對分析結果提出改進建議，協助審查委員將個人偏好影響評審分數的成分降低，以達到申請入學公平性。

（二）選才標準校正

本校交大校區於2017年創設「百川學士學位學程」（以下簡稱「百川」或「百川學程」），以特殊選材招生管道，希望招收具備「跨域學習」、「批判」、「創新」、「領導統御」、與「自主學習」等能力或有特殊專長之學生，為國家培育下一個世代知識創新、先驅／領袖型通才。百川學程的選才標準不採納大學學測或考試成績，主要透過書面資料審查（自傳、學習計畫等），以及筆試與面試選出以傳統學科考試無法衡量的特殊學習者與具有高度求知熱忱之學子。交大校區於今年110學年度即將迎來第四屆百川學子。百川學程由專家設計的課程模組，整合校內外資源以建立近乎個人化、彈性、跨學科、跨場域新型學習生態系統。此外，與校方協調供應宿舍促進學生建立同儕網絡，凝聚對學程之向心力與認同感。學程也邀請對教學有熱情且具有跨域背景與經驗之教授擔任百川導師，適時給予百川學子修業引導與關懷。

百川學程可謂本校引領台灣高教界發起之教育實驗。為檢視百川學程之運作，瞭解制度實施成果與學習成效，每年皆有教育領域專家與教授[7]針對百川學程實施教育評鑑。本校教育研究所吳俊育教授與其研究團隊針對第一屆百川學生進行面談筆試分析、學習成效，與評量整體學習適應程度（吳俊育、粘美玟、程姿螢，2020）。此外，本中心以半結構式一對一訪談為主及問卷調查為輔，從個人背景、學習特質、學業與修課經驗、生活、社交、與課外活動等方面，瞭解百川學生在學程中的學習與生活狀況。從問卷調查與訪談分析中發現，百川學生相較於其他一般大學生有著非常突出的學習特質，像是對自己在攻讀領域上的能力有較高的信心、學習上較具有獨立與主動性等，也特別會關注課程中是否有實際動

---

[7] 教育研究所陳昭秀與吳俊育教授，及大數據研究中心鄭朝陽教授在107學年度至109學年度有分別針對百川學程不同面向實施教育評鑑。

手做與應用所學的機會。

在百川學程修業規定中，最特別也最不可或缺的一環在於學生在每個學期都需要與指導教授合作下製作專題，累積學習成果，並在畢業專題上能整合過去學習經驗、展現學習成效。經由訪談發現，專題在部分學子眼中是幫助他們向前，並且給予他們相當多養分的訓練與活動。而專題導師正是帶著這群百川學子們探索、一展長才的領航者。我們觀察到學生們在訪談中經常提起專題導師，也有不少同學直接表示與專題導師很契合、在學習的過程中開啟了更多的想像。

由此可見，經由定期的學程評鑑研究，不僅提供資訊予以學程相關人員參考，也能作為未來特殊選才招生策略政策、修訂學程相關規定、與學程未來運作之依據。此外，針對百川學程學生的特質與個別差異的描述與資訊，也能夠幫助輔導諮商人員對百川學生有更深層的瞭解，未來能提供更適切的輔導與協助。

二、育才分析

本校在林奇宏校長的帶領下，提出「一樹百穫」計畫書[8]，擘劃十年願景三年策略。在「以終為始——突破框架的教育未來式」此章節，指出為因應教育4.0的潮流，跨域學習、目標導向學程、個人化學習歷程、國際流動等已成為未來高教關鍵趨勢。為了培養學生能面對未來複雜問題、自主學習，並能針對問題提出解決方案，高等教育的教學方式應從線性、單向、有秩序的講授方式，轉變成動態複雜，且相對模糊的方式。學習型態則需從過去的單一個領域的專業學習，轉變成具備「跨地域」（Trans-Locality）、「跨文化」（Cross-Cultural）、「跨領域」（Cross-Discipline），甚至是「跨世代」（Cross-Generation）等特性。

[8] 國立陽明交通大學「一樹百穫計畫」https://nycu-plan.tw/

為了培養學生擁有跨領域知識與跨領域合作的能力，本校自105學年度起開始實施「跨域學程」，鼓勵學生拓展第二專長。在不額外增加（或僅有少量增加）畢業學分數的原則下，透過彈性學分的設計，搭配系所核心課程的模組化，提供學生彈性學習空間。此外，本校也首創New Chiao Tung Upgraded – Innovative Creative Technology（NCTU-ICT工坊，亦稱創創工坊[9]）全校資源分享與交流平台，規劃具特色性、前瞻性與創新性的主題課程，讓全校學生都有機會學習新興科技與最新議題，體驗跨領域學習。創創工坊集結不同領域的教師，跳脫科系必選修藩籬，以領域小組與工作坊為基礎，首創彈性學分設計。創創工坊以實作課程為主軸，引導學生將理論與實作結合，並強調跨域交流、合作共創，設有核心實作與專業實作課程，及微學分課程與學習坊，提供學生彈性學習空間。

為培養兼具臨床醫師與科學研究能力與創新的生醫領袖人才，陽明校區於104學年度設有「醫師科學家組」（亦稱醫學系B組），招收對科學研究有高度熱忱的醫學生。醫師科學家組學生於大一大二接受「跨領域生醫人才培育」的基礎科學教育，之後進行論文研究，再銜接原有的醫學系實習課程，畢業可取得醫學士及碩士雙學位。同時，為培育兼具數位醫療產業技術研發、創業及領導能力之醫師，本校於109學年度首創「醫師工程師組」，由醫學院與電機學院合作，規劃六年「跨域雙專長課程」，提供紮實的電資與醫學專業領域課程。醫師工程師組學生於大一大二時在交大校區修習基礎醫學與電機資訊相關課程，大三後則回到陽明校區完成醫學系問題導向學習（Problem-Based Learning，簡稱PBL）與實習課程，畢業時可取得醫學士學位，同時具備電資雙專長。

2021年8月，本校更獲教育部審議通過，與台積電、鴻海等公司合作，串聯校內專業學院、研究中心、研發中心等，設立全國首

[9] 國立陽明交通大學創創工坊官方網頁：https://ict.nycu.edu.tw/

間「產學創新研究學院」，以產學共創的理念，與產業建立長期深化的合作關係，加強學術與產業界的連結，加速培育更多國際化產業菁英。同時，本校於110學年度啟動大學部「博雅書苑」（Liberal Arts College）推行博雅教育，培養學生跨域知能，具備人文、藝術和倫理的品格，且有能力並主動參與公共事務，關懷社會與環境。

本中心在各式新創學程、通識課程等從不缺席，以學生為中心，使用校務數據分析為基礎，幫助教師改進教學品質與建立學生學習成效評估機制，瞭解學生對於通識教育課程的態度與想法，已經協助本校在跨域學程與通識課程之推動成效進行相關研究分析：

（一）跨域學程之學習成效評估

為幫助教師改進教學品質與建立學生學習成效評估機制，自105學年度跨域學程創立以來，本中心不斷協助跨域學程教師針對學生學習狀況、跨領域制度與教學模式進行評估。研究發現，從105學年度至108學年度，跨域教師與學生人數逐年遞增；修習跨域學程學生學習動機強烈，其學業表現優於其他學制學生，且畢業後繼續升學比例高。整體而言，跨域學程提供的課程內容，能帶給學生充實有效的跨域學習經驗，且能產生持續學習的動力（張德磁、卓坤中，2020）。

（二）通識教育課程之態度與想法調查

本中心協助通識教育中心瞭解學生對於通識教育課程的態度與想法，針對「通識教育的定義」、「通識教育的目標」、「通識課程的評價」、「通識課程與專業課程的差異」、「通識教育的責任」、「通識課程的設計」、「通識課程的學習狀況」等主題進行探討。根據學生的填答結果，可以發現多數學生對於通識課程的評價、制度與學分安排等有著正向的評價；普遍認為通識課程確實能讓學生習得博雅知識、提升表達／溝通能力，甚至能夠透過修習不同領域的課程，不僅能夠認識更多朋友，也可以強化自身跨領域的能力。

本校過去，現在與將來，從不間斷的發展出許多新型跨領域教學與研究的創新模式，如何有效協助各教學與研究單位進行品質管控與循環改善，為重要且必須的課題。本中心也會持續以校務數據分析為基礎，以學生為中心，針對教師、學校、教學醫院／實習場域三方面進行校務議題評估，提供分析結果給予主責教學研究單位參考，以強化教學品質，協助政策擬定與推動。

三、展才分析

大專院校除了提供一個高品質的學習環境，使入學學生能夠適才適性的學習與發展專業之外，培養學生具備畢業後進入全球職場的競爭力與知識技能也是重要目標。根據法國Emerging人力資源諮詢公司進行的全球大專院校就業力排名報告[10]（Emerging, 2020）指出，影響大專院校就業力表現包含以下六個主要因素：

1. 學術表現（Academic performance）：精準選才、高品質的研究與教育
2. 專業度（Specialization）：最新科技與商業專業能力、專精的研究領域
3. 畢業技能（Graduate skills）：畢業生軟實力及數位素養
4. 工作專業（Focus on work expertise）：創業環境、產學／實習課程、企業合作夥伴
5. 數位表現（Digital performance）：線上學習平台、創新學習方法等

---

[10] 根據報告Global Employability Survey and Ranking 2020: Selected Results of the Survey。此六大因素是經由詢問參與調查者以下問題總結而來：Measuring both expectations of the corporate market（"What is important when selecting university partners"）and university performance（"What university is the best in this category?"）

6. 國際化程度（Internationality）：國際聲譽、外籍教師/國際化課程等

大專院校除了能精準找到興趣、志向、能力與校系相符的學生、提供與時俱進的課程與教學型態培養學生擁有專業的硬實力與軟實力之外，更須持續地針對學生的畢業流向及雇主滿意度進行評估，根據學生進入職場後的經驗以及雇主的回饋，發展符合職場所需的課程內容與活動，使得學生進入職場後擁有競爭力與所需的技能。

本中心持續協助各系所單位進行畢業生、學校、雇主等各方資料之校務研究，針對畢業生職涯規劃及個人專業成長的情形進行評估，瞭解就業力與職場表現與企業需求之一致性，提供各系所與單位能夠根據研究結果調整課程或是擬定更佳適合的政策。此外，本中心也定期評估畢業生的就業狀況，協助本校強化與產業之鏈結。

（一）畢業生流向調查

為瞭解畢業生畢業後之規劃，本中心與系所合作，針對畢業生流向進行較深入的研究。舉例來說，為瞭解某學院畢業生畢業後的規劃，瞭解人才培育成效，並進一步觀察是否可能存在人才外流之情形，根據問卷填答結果發現，許多畢業生畢業後多以就業、實習或求職為主要選擇，其次是升學。選擇「就業、實習、求職中」的畢業生，多數選擇留在台灣工作。選擇「升學」的畢業生，多數在畢業前皆已錄取國內研究所，少數學生選擇到國外繼續升學。此外，本中心也定期協助國際事務處瞭解國際學生畢業生涯意向，作為擬定輔導國際學生留台發展策略之參考方向。

（二）畢業生就業力分析

除了進行畢業生流向之校務研究外，本中心也關注國內外各機構針對大專院校進行的就業力排名，以掌握本校畢業生進入國內

外企業後能否學以致用，具備企業所需之技能。此外，本中心也會根據排名結果佐以校務資料進行綜合性評估，給予校方全方面的建議。舉例來說，根據Cheers雜誌公布2021年「企業最愛大學生調查」，本校畢業生在「專業知識與技術」、「創新能力」、「學習意願強、可塑性高」、「解決問題能力」、「抗壓性高」、「團隊合作」、「融會貫通能力」及「數位應用」等能力皆位居台灣前三名（陳建銘，2021）；遠見雜誌與104人力銀行合作所公布的「2021起薪最佳大學」大數據報告（謝明彧，2021），本校資訊學群畢業生起薪與台灣其他三所頂尖大學並列全台最高，顯示在工業4.0的時代，大資工時代興起，在近年各行各業積極數位轉型的趨勢下，確實帶動了畢業生薪資水漲船高。

國內就業相關調查有助於瞭解本校畢業生於國內的競爭力，但在全球化的環境下，學生畢業後的舞台則是在全世界。因此，除了掌握國內就業相關調查結果外，大專院校也更加重視國外的就業力排名結果。舉例來說，國外就業力排名有英國泰晤士報「全球大學就業排行榜」（Times Higher Education Global University Employability Ranking）及Quacquarelli Symonds「全球畢業生就業競爭力排名」（QS Graduate Employability Rankings），主要調查全球哪些大專院校的畢業生最具競爭力且受雇主重視。本校交大校區2017 QS全球畢業生就業競爭力排名落在151-200區間，2018位於161-170區間（此年排名區間變小），而在2019至2021排名，本校進步至全球第141-150名，國內排名第二。進步的主因在於，「雇主聲譽」（Employer Reputation）及「畢業生成就」（Alumni Outcomes）二項指標之得分逐年進步，顯示本校畢業生在各領域上皆表現優異，受到雇主重視，且在各領域能夠有良好的發展。

四、世界大學排名分析

"Rankings are looked by our respective students, our future students, our staff and our society, which conclude as to how successfully we are fulfilling our mission. Despite the visibility, it is my belief that we university leaders cannot be slaved by the rankings and their evolving methodologies; rather, we must have the confidence to do the best at our missions and hope the rankings successfully reflect our successes and failures. Noting each of our institutions, more than anything, universities going forward must place themselves at the epic center of society, guide the transformations that must occur to achieve a globally sustainable future. I believe the alternative, for me, is not worth contemplating."

~by **Brian Schmidt**（2018 THE Academy World Summit, Singapore）

為增加學校的國際能見度，大專院校皆會參與各項國際學術評級計畫，如QS世界大學排名（QS World University Rankings）、THE世界大學排名（THE World University Rankings）、及上海軟科教育信息諮詢有限公司（簡稱上海軟科）世界大學學術排名（Academic Ranking of World Universities）等，目的為瞭解大專院校整體及在各項教育研究評比指標上，與全球大專院校相比之表現，以發現學校的優劣勢。每年六月，先有QS世界大學排名、八月上海軟科世界大學學術排名，九月則是THE世界大學排名。當然，除了此三大排名系統外，還有其他國內外相當多不同規模及評量項目的排名系統，像是美國新聞與世界報導（U.S. News）每年公布的全球最佳大學排名、國立臺灣大學世界大學科研論文質量評比（NTU Performance Ranking of Scientific Papers for World Universities）等。除了針對大專院校整體教育研究表現進行評比之外，各排名系統也會於每年發布全球大專院校學科排名。

本中心作為本校智庫，除了檢視本校排名表現以及掌握國內外高教趨勢與變化之外，也需要針對各項教育研究指標進行綜合性分析，同時評估未來排名結果，提供校方關於校務、學務、教務、及研發等策略制定之回饋與參考。

（一）排名系統評比指標比較

QS、THE、上海軟科世界大學學術排名之三大排名系統所使用的各項評比指標與著重的部分皆不相同。根據學術論文資料庫、聲譽與學術表現、師生人數相關、國際化程度，及經費相關等類別，針對三大排名系統中使用的指標進行分類比校。由表2可知，QS與THE相當看重大專院校的聲譽表現，給予其相對較高的權重，而上海軟科學術排名可以說是只針對大專院校的學術表現與影響力、校友學術成就進行評比。此外，本中心也持續追蹤歷年本校在各項評比指標中的變化趨勢，除了可瞭解本校優劣勢外，亦可提供數據資料協助本校各教學、研究單位評估目前的教學與研究狀況、經費運用、升等辦法與獎勵制度、國際影響力等面向，提出強化本校於全球大專院校中的競爭力之未來策略。

（二）大學影響力排名分析

除了上述針對學術研究的排名系統外，THE於2019年發佈了大學影響力排名（THE Impact Rankings）。有別於過去以學術聲譽、教學、與研究為重點的排名系統，影響力排名以聯合國於2015年9月發表「2030年永續發展目標」（Sustainable Development Goals，簡稱SDGs）為架構，評估大專院校對社會與環境永續議題上產生的影響力。自THE發布大學影響力排名以來，全球高等教育機構紛紛響應。此舉不僅能督促政府持續推動與落實國家永續發展目標，也能重新檢視高等教育機構對於在地社會與全球社群的影響力。

表2　THE、QS、上海軟科世界大學排名指標定義比較

評比系統	QS WORLD UNIVERSITY RANKINGS	THE WORLD UNIVERSITY RANKINGS	ACADEMIC RANKING OF WORLD UNIVERSITIES
論文資料來源	Scopus	Scopus	WOS
聲譽表現	學術聲譽(40%) 雇主聲譽(10%)	教學聲譽(15%) 研究聲譽(18%)	無
聲譽問卷	學術聲譽：*不可*投任職學校、 國外票數有較高權重(85:15) 雇主聲譽：國內外票數權重50:50	THE 學者名單(資料庫提供)：Targets only experienced/senior, published scholars 收到問卷之學者可提名15所大學，*可*投任職學校， 並無指出國外票數有較高權重	無
學術表現	論文師均被引用次數(20%) 扣除Self-Citation (同一機構內的引用皆視為Self-Citation)	師均論文數(6%) 領域權重引用影響力指數(30%)-論文引用次數佔類似論文之平均引用次數之比值 未扣除Self-Citation	獲Nobel/Fields獎校友數(10%) 獲Nobel/Fields獎教師數(20%) 高被引學者人數(20%) Nature及Science論文數(20%) SCIE/SSCI論文數(20%)
研究論文參採類型	Article, review, conference paper, book, book chapter, article in press, business article	Journal articles, article reviews, conference proceedings, books and book chapters	僅限Article類型
生師人數相關	生師比(20%)	共12.75%：含生師比(4.5%) 博士/學士授予學位人數比(2.25%) 博士學位授予人數/教師數(6%)	師均表現(10%)
國際化程度	國際教師比例(5%) 國際學生比例(5%)	國際教師比例(2.5%) 國際學生比例(2.5%) 國際著作比例(2.5%)	無
經費相關	無	校務總收入/教師數(2.25%) 師均研究經費(6%) 師均產學收入(2.5%)	無

本文作者自行整理

根據THE官方公告，2021年有近98個國家／地區，1,240所大學參加影響力排名，而台灣也有35所大專院校參與。THE影響力排名系統參酌大專院校在每一個永續發展目標上的研究能量與影響力，同時也評估大專院校在各永續發展目標上之政策制定、活動與服務、延續性指標（例如：永續發展目標3—良好健康與社會福祉，以大專院校培養獲得與醫學健康相關學位畢業生數量為其中之一指標項目），及組織治理等層面上的表現，使用非學術性質的證據與數據作為評比資料。

檢視THE影響力排名的目的與內涵，不難發現，實質上與教育部推行大學社會責任（University Social Responsibility，簡稱USR）實踐之宗旨不謀而合。教育部於2017年推動「大學社會責任實踐計畫」（亦稱USR計畫）（教育部大學社會責任推動中心，無日期），並於2018年連結「高教深耕計畫」啟動第一期USR計畫，

鼓勵大專院校在培育未來人才的同時，兼顧在地發展，並以三個面向進行創新與突破：（1）提升與地方社會的互動與連結以解決區域問題，促進在地創生與在地產業發展；（2）展開跨領域、跨科系、跨校結合，培育符合社會發展需求、具有創新能力的人才；（3）提升善盡社會責任的意識，發展學校特色（郭耀煌，2019）。而在USR第二期（2020-2022年）計畫中，教育部明確指出接軌聯合國永續發展目標為計畫審查重點要素之一，鼓勵大專院校以執行USR計畫之經驗與國際對接（唐鳳，2019）。USR以在地連結為核心，鼓勵大專院校帶動在地產業發展、連結學校資源協助城鄉教育發展、促進在地就業，這些內涵其實都能與永續發展目標很多項目與指標有所對應。

作為本校永續發展與創新主責單位，本中心也定期彙整本校各單位與永續發展相關質量化資料、維護永續發展成果網站與出版年度永續發展年報，以作為和利害關係人之溝通平台與工具，強化本校與國際之連結性及影響力。同時，本中心也利用校務倉儲資料盤點各學院及單位歷年所開設之課程，發現本校開設的課程涵蓋所有17項永續發展目標，且各學院與單位開設之課程內容與永續發展目標之間的連結與其訂定之教育目標與核心能力相當一致。此外，透過分析2016年至2020年本校在永續發展目標上的研究成果，發現本校在「永續發展目標5—性別平等」上，雖五年內論文產出數僅69篇，被引用總次數卻高達5,872次，領域權重影響力指數（Field weighted citation impact，簡稱FWCI）達10.18（代表該領域的引用影響力比全球平均高出918%），充分顯示了本校在性別平等相關研究領域上的影響力。此外，為了呈現本校與各院於永續議題上之成果，本中心也歸納校級與院級與永續議題相關之教研與行政業務上之亮點，除建置校級永續發展目標公開網站外，也協助各院建置永續發展目標成果網頁。透過蒐集各單位執行亮點，協助宣傳本校於永續發展目標上之耕耘成效。

伍、未來展望

如前所述，面對教育4.0所帶來的教育制度與學習型態的轉變，大學作為國家產業人才培育的重要機構，必須與時俱進，掌握產業發展趨勢以及人才需求，瞭解產業所需人才應具備哪些能力及專長經驗，進而調整學校的各項課程規劃及學習制度的修正。同時，為瞭解並掌握學校所提供的彈性修課制度、創新課程模式（例如：跨域學程、問題導向學習課程、自主學習等）以及學校選才、育才、展才等面向之實施成效。校務研究單位作為大學的智庫，必須持續針對各項校務研究議題進行資料蒐集與分析，將研究結果進行闡釋並提出相關建議給予學校各單位作為政策修正或學校發展方向之參考。尤其在經歷COVID-19疫情之後，大學教育將面臨全球教育型態與模式的轉變，加上工業4.0發展出的新興科技與資訊技術應用，讓大學必須持續思考如何透過校務研究掌握並瞭解學校推動教育4.0時於各項學習制度及課程規劃，甚至是招生制度與學生畢業後的發展等的推動成效，同時也應即時掌握產業發展趨勢以及人才需求，時時檢視學校所培育出來的學生，是否都已具備足夠的重要關鍵能力，以因應未來產業所需。

順應教育4.0的浪潮，大學必須做好充足準備，並應著手規劃面對未來教與學的挑戰，而隨著學校變得更加智慧化，校務研究除了執行常規性與探索性議題之外，也將以戰略性角度思考校務資料在推動創新教育學制以及新型態教學模式時所扮演的角色，或是針對校園環境、職能領域、學術研究、教學活動等方面，如何透過校務資料亦或是蒐集哪些資料數據及統計分析，可有效洞察校務發展情形，進而輔助學校領導者進行決策。對此，我們提出以下建議，期能作為面對教育4.0，校務研究仍能持續扮演協助學校思考、規劃與決策時的智庫，提供實證數據協助學校決策者作為改善與創新行政與教學等決策之依據。

一、完善校務大數據數位治理決策環境

藉由數位科技應用，持續精進校務資料管理基礎架構，發展以數據為中心的校務決策環境與能力。建立校園內資料治理及分析利用概念，打造校務資料利用生態，並強化校務資料收集、整合與循環活化利用；利用校務資料研究校務發展，掌握國際高等教育改變之脈動與產業趨勢，持續發展以學生為中心的校務研究議題，以協助校務數位治理與教育品質管控；並強化各單位自主管理及分析利用的能力，推動以數據為證的政策擬定、推動與評估。

二、推動校園資料加值與分析應用

以校務資料管理架構為核心，擴大校內資料蒐集與利用，推動建立校園資料入口，廣納校內行政、產學、研究、教學等各類資料集，鼓勵各行政與學研單位資料釋出，以提供跨領域資料整合與大數據分析、人工智慧等多元利用，藉此活化各類型資料的流動與加值應用；由資料管理與平台提供者的角度，提供各領域資料釋出的平台，建立資料市集服務，提供資料交換與分析等資源，以降低資料流通的門檻，並形成校園資料分析應用的循環生態體系。

三、建立校園永續發展實踐社會影響力

台灣2030年科技願景為「實現創新、包容、永續」，發展六大核心產業—資訊及數位、資安、生物及醫療科技、民生及戰備產業、綠電及再生能源、國防及戰略產業。結合學校本身的發展特色與強項（例如：半導體、電子資訊、醫學照護、農業科技、師資

培育等），配合國家政策回應國家需求，以「在地連結、區域合作、科技創新」為基礎，於優質教育、研究創新、學校治理、社會參與等四個層面，積極推動大學社會實踐，接軌國際夥伴共同促進永續發展（SDGs），協助學校培育更多優秀人才，持續發揮大學影響力與善盡社會責任，共同承擔社會、經濟、環境永續發展之責任。

參考文獻

Bujang, S. D. A., Selamat, A., Krejcar, O., Maresova, P., & Nguyen, N. T. (2020). Digital learning demand for future Education 4.0—Case studies at Malaysia education institutions. *Informatics, 7*(2), 13. https://www.mdpi.com/2227-9709/7/2/13

Deaconu, A., Dedu, E. M., Igreț, R. Ș., & Radu, C. (2018). The use of information and communications technology in vocational education and training—Premise of sustainability. *Sustainability, 10*(5), 1466. https://www.mdpi.com/2071-1050/10/5/1466

Demartini, C., & Benussi, L. (2017). Do Web 4.0 and Industry 4.0 imply Education X.0? *IT Professional, 19*(3), 4-7. https://doi.org/10.1109/MITP.2017.47

Emerging. (2020). *Global employability survey and ranking 2020: Selected results of the survey.* https://emerging.fr/#/geurs2020

Frank, A. G., Dalenogare, L. S., & Ayala, N. F. (2019). Industry 4.0 technologies: Implementation patterns in manufacturing companies. *International Journal of Production Economics, 210*, 15-26. https://doi.org/10.1016/j.ijpe.2019.01.004

Harkins, A. M. (2008). Leapfrog principles and practices: Core components of education 3.0 and 4.0. *Futures Research Quarterly, 24*(1), 19-31. http://www.filosofiacienciaarte.org/attachments/article/1128/HarkinsCoreComponents.pdf

Hien, H. T., Cuong, P.-N., Nam, L. N. H., Nhung, H. L. T. K., & Thang, L. D. (2018). *Intelligent assistants in higher-education environments: The FIT-EBot, a chatbot for administrative and learning support.* Proceedings of the Ninth International Symposium on Information and Communication Technology, Danang City,

VietNam. https://doi.org/10.1145/3287921.3287937

Hussin, A. A. (2018). Education 4.0 made simple: Ideas for teaching. *International Journal of Education and Literacy Studies, 6*(3), 92-98. https://doi.org/10.7575/aiac.ijels.v.6n.3p.92

IBM. (n.d.). *What is Industry 4.0?* https://www.ibm.com/topics/industry-4-0

IBM. (2021). *2021 CEO Study: Find your essential.* https://www.ibm.com/downloads/cas/WVPWGPYE

Iyer, A. (2018). Moving from Industry 2.0 to Industry 4.0: A case study from India on leapfrogging in smart manufacturing. *Procedia Manufacturing,* 21, 663-670. https://doi.org/10.1016/j.promfg.2018.02.169

JISC. (2019). *Horizons report on emerging technologies and education.* https://repository.jisc.ac.uk/7284/1/horizons-report-spring-2019.pdf

Kazimirov, A. N. (2018, November 13-15). *Education at university and Industry 4.0.* 2018 Global Smart Industry Conference(GloSIC), Chelyabinsk, Russia.

Kenneth, S. R. (2012). *Essential scrum: A practical guide to the most popular agile process.* Addison-Wesley Professional.

Kramer, I. (2017, July 7-8). *Creating employment opportunities for everybody through dynamic labor markets and a global level playing field for fair competition.* G20 GERMANY 2017. https://digital.thecatcompanyinc.com/g20magazine/may-2017/ingo-kramer/

Kunnari, I., Tien, T. H., & Nguyen, T.-L. (2019). Rethinking learning towards Education 4.0. *HAMK Unlimited Journal.* https://unlimited.hamk.fi/ammatillinen-osaaminen-ja-opetus/rethinking-learning-education-4-0

Lee, J., Bagheri, B., & Kao, H.-A. (2015). A cyber-physical systems architecture for Industry 4.0-based manufacturing systems. *Manufacturing Letters, 3,* 18-23. https://doi.org/10.1016/j.mfglet.2014.12.001

Leonard-Barton, D. A. (1998). *Wellsprings of knowledge.* Harvard Business School Press. https://www.hbs.edu/faculty/Pages/item.aspx?num=73

OECD. (2017). *OECD skills strategy diagnostic report: Netherlands.* https://www.oecd.org/skills/nationalskillsstrategies/OECD-Skills-Strategy-Diagnostic-Report-Netherlands.pdf

OECD. (2018). *The future of education and skills: Education 2030.* https://www.oecd.org/education/2030/E2030%20Position%20Paper%20(05.04.2018).pdf

Salmon, G. (2019). May the fourth be with you: Creating Education 4.0. *Journal of Learning for Development,, 6*(2), 95-115. http://files.eric.ed.gov/fulltext/EJ1222907.pdf

Schwab, K. (2016). *The Fourth Industrial Revolution: What it means, how to respond.* https://www.weforum.org/agenda/2016/01/the-fourth-industrial-revolution-what-it-means-and-how-to-respond

Sinlarat, P. (2016). *Education 4.0 is more than education.* Annual Academic Seminar of the Teacher's Council on the Topic of Research of the Learning Innovation and Sustainable Educational Management, Bangkok, Thailand.

Vandervelde, W. (2021). *WINGS: The 5 primary skills for the future of work.* https://waltervandervelde.medium.com/wings-the-5-primary-skills-for-the-future-of-work-461d128e23fc

Villegas-Ch, W., Arias-Navarrete, A., & Palacios-Pacheco, X. (2020). Proposal of an architecture for the integration of a chatbot with artificial intelligence in a smart campus for the improvement of learning. *Sustainability, 12*(4), 1500. https://www.mdpi.com/2071-1050/12/4/1500

Sarma, S., & Yoquinto, L. (2021). *Grasp: The science transforming how we learn.* Doubleday.

The World Economic Forum. (2020). *Schools of the future: Defining new models of education for the Fourth Industrial Revolution.* https://www.weforum.org/reports/schools-of-the-future-defining-new-models-of-education-for-the-fourth-industrial-revolution

Xing, B. (2019). Towards a magic cube framework in understanding higher Education 4.0 for the Fourth Industrial Revolution. In D. B. A. Khosrow-Pou (Ed.), *Handbook of research on challenges and opportunities in launching a technology driven international university* (pp. 107-130). IGI Global.

王蒞君、劉奕蘭（2020）。**化鏡為窗：大數據分析強化大學競爭力**。國立陽明交通大學出版社。

吳俊育、粘美玫、程姿螢（2021）。百川學子引領自學新潮流。王蒞君、劉奕蘭（主編），**化鏡為窗：大數據分析強化大學競爭力**（頁14-37）. 國立陽明交通大學出版社。

洪詠善（2016）。學習趨勢：跨領域、現象為本的統整學習。**國家教育研究院電子報**，134。https://epaper.naer.edu.tw/edm.php?grp_no=2&edm_no=134&content_no=2671

唐鳳（2019）。**從大學社會責任實踐計畫與聯合國永續發展目標連結看未來發展趨勢與策略**。https://usr.moe.gov.tw/blog/25409

張繐磁、卓坤申（2020）。校務研究助攻破解跨領域成功密碼。王蒞君、劉奕蘭（主編），**化鏡為窗：大數據分析強化大學競爭力**（頁66-86）。國立陽明交通大學出版社。

教育部（2014）。**十二年國民基本教育課程綱要—總綱**。https://www.naer.edu.tw/ezfiles/0/1000/attach/87/pta_18543_581357_62438.pdf

教育部大學招生委員會聯合會（2019）。**大學考招新方案與銜接配套措施**。https://12basic.edu.tw/assets/file/ppt/%E5%A4%A7%E5%AD%B8%E8%80%83%E6%8B%9B%E9%80%A3%E5%8B%95%E5%AE%A3%E5%B0%8E.pdf

教育部大學社會責任推動中心（無日期）。**關於USR計畫：聚焦社會議題，實踐永續發展**。https://usr.moe.gov.tw/about-1

教育部高教司（2018）。**大學招生專業化發展試辦計畫**。https://www.ntue.edu.tw/File/Userfiles/0000000001/files/1070529%E9%99%84%E4%BB%B61_%E5%A4%A7%E5%AD%B8%E6%8B%9B%E7%94%9F%E5%B0%88%E6%A5%AD%E5%8C%96%E7%99%BC%E5%B1%95%E8%A9%A6%E8%BE%A6%E8%A8%88%E7%95%AB_%E8%AA%AA%E6%98%8E%E6%9C%83%E7%B0%A1%E5%A0%B1_.pdf

郭耀煌（2020）。**春芽：大學社會參與的萌發與茁壯：聚積與連結**。教育部大學

陳建銘（2021）。2021企業最愛大學生：台大重回冠軍，「解決力」是人才勝出關鍵。**Cheers雜誌**。https://www.cheers.com.tw/career/article/5098880

彭森明（2019）。**高等教育校務研究的理念與應用**。高教出版。

鄭朝陽、林珊如（2020）。大數據精準招生開展共贏局面。王蒞君、劉奕蘭（主編），**化鏡為窗：大數據分析強化大學競爭力**（頁88-107）。

國立陽明交通大學出版社。
謝明彧（2021）。【獨家】哪個系所最鍍金？遠見「2021起薪最佳大學」大數據報告。**遠見雜誌**。https://www.gvm.com.tw/article/77860

Higher Education Internationalization in Indonesia: Opportunities and Challenges
印尼高等教育國際化推動之研究：機會與挑戰

Iis Nur Rodliyah, Syariful Muttaqin, Ching-Hui Lin
National Sun Yat-sen University, Taiwan

因應高等教育全球化的趨勢，大學排名已經是全球高等教育品質保證的認可指標之一，印尼政府為了回應這樣的趨勢啟動建設全國性世界大學計畫，計畫期程從2015至2019共計四年，計畫預期補助印尼的五所頂尖大學進入世界五百大大學排名。基於此，本研究旨在（1）檢視印尼高等教育機構在大學排名系統的研究發表及國際合作指標情形；（2）分析印尼高等教育機構在邁向頂尖大學國際化的目標時，所面臨到的機會與挑戰。因此，本研究採用趨勢分析（trend analysis）檢視印尼高等教育機構的研究發表、國際合作及國內大學評鑑認可的情形，數據資料來源包括SciVal資料庫、Quacquarelli Symonds 世界大學排名（QS WUR）與印尼高等教育資料庫。

本研究結果發現印尼政府所補助的五所頂尖大學其研究發表數量原超過全國的目標值，甚至是東南亞國家中最高的，然而文章的引用率數值卻遠遠的落後於文章發表篇數。直至2019年，國內則有九十六所大學達到大學評鑑認可的A等級，QS世界大學排名僅有三所學校進入世界五百大大學排名。然而有些大學表現有其顯著的成長，預期可以在不久的未來進入世界五百大大學排名。整體而言，政府對於高等教育經費的挹注顯示出QS世界大學排名不如預期的表現，因此，本研究建議高等教育機構可加以強化重要指標如校務治理系統、人力資源編制、國際合作。因此，藉由大學排名指標揭示了對於高等教育機構整體排名尚須改進的地方，本文亦針對五所被選定的頂尖大學對於在大學排名指標中強化學校聲譽所面臨到的機會與挑戰有更多的著墨與討論。

1. Introduction

The number or higher education internationalization activities has been growing significantly in the past two decades (Altbach & Knight, 2007). This has been indicated by the global academic mobility shown by a significant number of students going abroad to pursue overseas study in order to obtain a foreign degree and the increasing quantity of universities that open overseas campus branches in other countries to accommodate local students getting education and degree from a reputable international higher education institution without necessarily going abroad. The motivations for such internationalization can range from being profit-oriented, that is earning money because of access provision and demand absorption, to nonprofit orientation, that is to enhance research and knowledge capacity and to increase cultural understanding, competitiveness, prestige, and strategic alliances of the university (Altbach & Knight, 2007). Some Asian countries have initiated their internationalization programs using different names, such as in Japan with the "Top global University Project (TGUP)" (Macaro et al., 2017), in Korea with BK 21, in Taiwan with "World class University Project (WCUP) (Fu, et al., 2020), and in Indonesia with World Class University (WCU) program.

One among the indicators of being successful in their internationalization is the universities' intended position in the world university ranking (WUR) as measured by external ranking organizations like the Times Higher Education (THE), Shanghai Jiao Tong University (SJTU) or the Shanghai Jiao Tong Academic Ranking of World Universities (ARWU), Webometrics, and QS World University Rankings (Hazelkorn, 2011; Liu et al., 2011). Many universities use the term World Class University (WCU) program to refer to the efforts for boosting their international reputations by applying different strategies that incorporate academic, research and publication, collaboration, and employability.

Both the central government and universities have reported facing some challenges in achieving the world class university (WCU) program goals. The challenges are heightening considering that the competition among universities has shifted from national or regional competition to the global one. In the global society, the competition among universities in both qualitative and quantitative aspects aim mainly at attracting external resources like potential students, professors, research funding, and other relevant stakeholders, into certain higher education institutions (Shin & Kehm, 2013). Lo and Hou (2019), based on their study conducted in Taiwan, emphasized the importance of national policy in the process of building world class universities. They argued that a reorientation of policy indicates the fundamental shift in higher education internationalization in Taiwan. They further clarified that the initiation of the global trend of building world class universities has been affecting the provision of universities long term-strategies that promote internationalization dimensions.

Globally, national policy on World Class University (WCU) projects has been adopted by many countries in their effort to both encourage and provide supports to several selected higher education institutions to be more internationally competitive and reputable (Mok, 2011). In determining the indicator of the WCU projects accomplishment, several national policies have been observed to refer to external agencies publishing the world university ranking. For example, in Taiwan, Fu et al. (2020) mentioned that the initial goal of Taiwan's WCU project had been to invest a massive amount of resources on a few best universities in order to send at least one of them to the world's top 100 and then top 50 within ten and twenty years respectively. Two Indonesian neighboring countries, Singapore and Malaysia, have also been showcasing prominent higher education institutions' (HEIs) performance internationally as a result of each country's governments initiation in promoting world class university that was started much earlier than in Indonesia. Singapore, through their Ministry of Education (MOE) has initiated the HEIs management reformation to its top universities as early as 2005 targeting the National University of Singapore (NUS) and Nanyang Technological University (NTU), and the Singapore Management University (SMU), while Malaysia has publicized their Ministry of Higher Education (MOHE) policies of the *National Higher Education Strategic Plan 2020* and the *National Higher Education Action Plan 2010* since August 2007 (Mok, 2011).

As a big developing country with 270,20 million population, Indonesia hosts 4,593 (122 public, 3,044 private, 187 ministerial/ government, and 1,240 religious) higher education institutions (HEIs) (Directorate General of Higher Education, 2020), comprising 35,913 study programs, 296,305 faculties or lecturers, and 8,870,714 students (PDDIKTI, 2021). To assure the quality of study programs, accreditation has been implemented by using criteria of A, B, and C from the highest to the lowest respectively. Of the total number of institutions, 4.373 have been accredited A (22.61%) (Directorate General of Higher Education, 2020). Along with the increasing trend in HE Internationalization, the Ministry of Education and Culture (MoEC) of the

Republic of Indonesia has initiated the WCU project since 2015 (Renstra DIKTI, 2015-2019). One of the indicators is that by the year 2019, five Indonesian universities should be in the top 500 WUR. The programs to support the achievement of this goal are increased relevance, quantity, and quality of HEI, increased capacity of science, technology, and innovation, and conducting bureaucracy reformation with specific key performance indicators (KPI) to be achieved by the end of 2019 (Renstra DIKTI, 2015).

The trend of world class university as indicated by global university rankings becomes consideration of Indonesian universities following their counterparts in Asian region leading to a more serious initiation to promote World Class University (WCU) achievement among Indonesian HEIs. In 2015, Indonesian Ministry of Research, Technology and Higher Education (MoRTHE) explicitly stated the goal of their WCU program was to have eleven selected public universities to achieve at least the 500th positions at QS world university ranking. The government of Indonesia then also allocated a significant amount of national budget for funding the WCU program as much IDR 7,200,000,000 annually for the 2015-2019 periods. Indonesian government regulation to build World Class University is intended to increase the global competitiveness of Indonesian HEIs (Dewi, 2018). She further mentioned that World Class University program in Indonesia comes with the expectation for increasing, among others, the excellences in teaching, research, international reputations, innovation, and collaboration (Dewi, 2018).

According to the 2015 OECD/ADB data and Times Higher Education, until 2015, not a single university in Indonesia is ranked in the top 500 World University Rankings (Jarvis & Mok, 2019). Thus, in 2015, the Indonesian Ministry of Research, Technology, and Higher Education (MoRTHE) initiated the World Class University (WCU) program and determined a set of targets to be achieved within the 5-year-period of 2015-2019. The government also mandated a few public universities to undergo the 2015-2019 WCU program. Initially, only Indonesian top 3 public universities were mandated to participate in Indonesian national WCU program in 2015 and the number, then, has been gradually increased to eleven top public universities by 2019. Based on the decree of Indonesian MoRTHE No. 50 year 2017 about the *Strategic Plan of the Ministry of Research, Education, and Technology 2015-2019,* among the specific goals set to improve the quality and competitiveness of Indonesian HEIs in both national and global levels are as presented in the following Table 1.

Table 1 The Indicators of Selected National and Global Performance of Indonesian HEIs 2015-2019

Activity Performance Indicators	The Targeted Number(Cumulative)				
	2015	2016	2017	2018	2019
National Competitiveness The number of HEIs accredited A by Indonesian BAN-PT	29	39	59	80	110
Global Competitiveness The number of HEIs selected and supported in the program of the Global WUR Top 500	-	3	3	4	5
The number of HEIs listed in the Global WUR Top 500	2	3	4	4	5

Note. The allotted budget for WCUP annually is IDR 7,200,000,000 (MoRTHE, 2017 pp 101, 108). MoRTHE

However, the performance indicator of Indonesian national world class university program as shown in the Table 1 has not been fully achieved yet in which by the end of 2019 only three instead of five universities were enlisted in the Top 500 of the QS WUR. The result indicates that both Indonesian government and HEIs managements need to work harder while at the same time to carefully identify the strength and weaknesses of and the potentials and hindrances faced by HEIs in Indonesia, so that both the government and the HEIs managements could plan more effective strategies to achieve the goal.

In line with the situation faced by Indonesian government and HEIs in their efforts for internationalization and for earning international reputation, the main objective of this article is to evaluate the performance of the selected top universities after their intensive work toward internationalization of higher education institutions (HEIs) in Indonesia within the timeline period of 2015-2019. This study specifically aims at finding the answers to the following two research questions:

1. How have research, publication, and collaboration of Indonesian HEIs impacted their world university ranking?
2. What implications do the potential opportunities and challenges have on Indonesian HEIs in achieving the national goals for internationalization?

This study is worthwhile doing considering that internationalization effort of HEIs through national world class university program requires numerous managerial and financial resources that can be among the limitations for developing countries, like Indonesia, that usually have less resources than those of developed countries. Therefore, the findings resulted from analyzing the challenges and opportunities faced by Indonesian government and its HEIs in establishing world class universities are significant in providing initial relevant insight on the whole picture of the given matter as well as the potential strategies to be adopted.

2. Literature Review

2.1. Higher Education Institution (HEI)

Internationalization

Those who are either interested in or having been working on WCU projects should be familiar with the statement delivered by Altbach (2004) mentioning that although establishing a WCU is desirable to any relevant parties, there has been no clear definition nor clear procedures or strategies to achieve one. This statement is further translated by Lee (2013) as there will be two important steps to consider for any authorities who want to build WCU (a) understanding the characteristics of WCUs and (b) understanding the concept and determining how to create one. Different countries might face different challenges as well as possess different strength in assisting their home HEIs having the quality and being recognized as WCUs.

Government policy makers or HEIs could refer to a specific framework for understanding the development of a WCU developed by Lee (2013) that focuses on the characteristic, challenges of both macro- and micro-levels, and what can be done by any specific HEIs and put these aspects in the relevant national and institutional contexts. Based on Lee's framework, the macro-level refers to the national situation and policy that can influence the establishment of WCUs in a country which most of the times become a national goal for HEIs reform agenda and a key for national development (Sadlak & Liu, 2009; Salmi, 2009; Wang, 2001 in Lee, 2013). While at the institutional level or micro-level of each individual university, achieving the WCU goal, especially for universities in developing countries are considered financially and administratively burdensome. Also, the research capacity and autonomy are relatively lower than those in more developed countries. However, when achieved, "at the institution level, WCUs are mechanisms that reinforce a country's capacity to compete in the global higher education market by acquiring, adapting, and creating advanced knowledge" (Salmi &Liu, 2011 in Lee, 2013).

2.2. World University Rankings in Indonesian World Class University Program Context

In the global society, the competition among universities in both qualitative and quantitative aspects aims mainly at attracting external resources like potential students, professors, research funding, and other relevant stakeholders, into certain higher education institutions (Shin & Kehm, 2013). This situation, then, forces both government and individual higher education institution to make their best internationalization efforts in order to become more competitive by gaining international reputation. Globally, national policy on World Class University (WCU) projects has been adopted by many countries in their effort to both encourage and provide supports to several selected higher education institutions to be more internationally competitive and reputable.

In determining the indicator of the WCU projects accomplishment, several national policies have been observed to refer to external agencies publishing the world university ranking. According to Hazelkorn (2011), using tables produced by ranking agencies as references are considered as convenient because it is the agencies who collect the data based on carefully developed indicators to compare HEIs. Nowadays, there have been several external accreditation agencies that have been globally acknowledged, for example, the Times Higher Education (THE), Shanghai Jiao Tong University

(SJTU) or the Shanghai Jiao Tong Academic Ranking of World Universities (ARWU), Webometrics, and QS World University Rankings (Hazelkorn, 2011; Liu et al., 2011).

Among the available world university rankings, Indonesian government has decided to use QS WUR as the main indicator for the successfulness of National World Class University program. In their Strategic Plan 2015-2019 document, Indonesian Ministry of Research, Technology, and Higher Education (MoRTHE) has clearly stated about the initiation of five-year-term World Class University Program 2015-2019 aiming at sending five out of eleven participating Indonesian public universities into Top 500 of QS WUR by the end of the program (MoRTHE, 2017). Therefore, the world class university concept and framework applied in Indonesian HEIs context automatically refer to the indicator metrics created by QS WUR publisher that consist of: Academic Reputation (40%), Employer Reputation (10%), Faculty/Student Ratio (20%), Citations per Faculty (20%), International Faculty Ratio (5%), and International Student Ratio (5%) (https://www.topuniversities.com/qs-world-university-rankings/methodology).

2.3. The Impact of Research, Publication, and Collaboration on University Rankings

Previous studies have proven the significance of research performance or outputs to the achievement of internationalization and higher position in Global WUR. While, some others, show that the research outputs and citations are higher when research collaborations take place. For example, N.K. et al. (2018) study found that in India, the universities who gained high scores for research productivity came top in NIRF (National Institutional Ranking Framework) as well as in world university rankings.

In another research, Cartes-Velásquez and Manterola (2017) show that a positive and significant correlation exists between research methodological quality and number of authors and between the methodological quality and countries. Furthermore, funding and collaboration are also found to influence the research performance in China and the USA, two countries having significant numbers of universities at the top Global WUR, at various impacting levels or degrees (Zhou & Cai, 2018). Zhou and Cai (2018) also revealed that collaboration also has impacts on the number of citations that also becomes an indicator used in many Global WUR assessments.

Another case study presents evidence that university research productivity and impact through collaboration is traceable. By utilizing a knowledge management model, research collaboration can be increased and eventually boosted a university's number of publications and citations (Ceballos at al., 2017). Thus, studying the research performance and research collaboration conducted by HEIs should be worth doing as this might help identifying better and more effective strategies in achieving the goal of WCU program.

In Indonesian higher education context, despite both the government and the university's policy and effort in increasing the numbers of publication in internationally reputable journals, the publication performance remains low (Alimi & Rokhman, 2017) and during the period of 2014-2019, the number of publications has even decreased within the period of 2018-2019 after previously experienced a significant rise (Nandiyanto et al., 2020). Another study on publication, research collaboration, and citation performance conducted on Indonesian top universities have shown similar phenomena of considerably lower performance compared to that other countries in the region, especially Singapore and Malaysia (Darmadji et al., 2018). Furthermore, Darmadji et al. (2018) pointed out that as part of efforts in achieving world class university, appropriate or on point policy and strategy regulating research collaboration in all levels, not only international, but also regional and national ones might contribute significantly and efficiently on the rise of research, publication, and citation performance.

2.4. Indonesian Higher Education in a Nutshell

According to data released by the Secretariat Directorate General of Higher Education of Indonesia (2020), being among the countries with the highest number of populations in the world, by 2020, Indonesia hosts as many as 4,593 higher education institutions (HEIs) to serve 8,483,213 students (Directorate General of Higher Education, 2020). The 4,593 Indonesian HEIs take six different institutional forms and can be categorized in two criteria based on the form of education and the supervising group. The followings three paragraphs are the brief details of Indonesian HEIs system that are extracted from the publication of *Higher Education Statistical Year Book 2020* published by the Secretariat Directorate General of Higher Education of Indonesia (2020).

The six forms or types of Indonesian HEIs and their corresponding institutional numbers are (1) *Universitas* (University), 667 institutions; (2) *Institut* (Institute), 271 institutions; (3) *Sekolah Tinggi* (School of Higher Learning), 2.465 institutions; (4) *Akademi* (Academy), 830 institutions, (5) *Akademi Komunitas* (Community College), 38 institutions; and (5) *Politeknik* (Polytechnic), 322 institutions. Regarding the Form of Education, these six kinds of HEIs can be classified into either *Pendidikan Tinggi Akademik* (Academic Higher Education) or *Pendidikan Tinggi Vokasi* (Vocational Higher Education). The majority of Indonesian HEIs fall under the Academic Higher Education category with 3, 403 institutions, while the rest or 1,190 others belong to the Vocational one. The main difference between these two forms is that the former category is higher education undergraduate and/or postgraduate programs aimed at mastering and developing branches of science and technology, while the latter refers to higher education diploma programs that prepare students for jobs with specific applied skills and to prepare students for applied undergraduate and postgraduate programs.

Depending on the Supervising Group, Indonesian HEIs are classified into four types: (1) *Perguruan Tinggi Negeri (PTN)* or Public Higher Education. This refers to HEIs that are established and/or organized by the government (122 institutions); (2) *Perguruan Tinggi Swasta (PTS)* or Private Higher Education is HEIs that are established and/or organized by public (3,044 institutions); (3) *Perguruan Tinggi Agama (PTA)* or Religious Higher Education Institutions refers to HEIs that organize religious higher education (1,240 institutions); and (4) *Perguruan Tinggi Kedinasan (PTK/L)* or Government Higher Education Institution is all HEIs that are established and/or organized by the government specific institutions like a Ministry or National Defense Force institution and whose graduate are to be recruited to work for the given *PTK/L* (187 institution). Among the four, the first and the second categories, i.e., Public and Private HEIs, are under the supervision of Indonesian Ministry of Education (MoEC), the third HEI category is under Indonesian Ministry of Religion Affairs, and the fourth category is under the supervision of the relevant government ministries, bureaus, or agencies.

Based on the data from the 2020 Indonesian Higher education statistics, the total number or enrolled students who are distributed in 29,413 various HEIs' study programs is 8,483,213 students. In 2020, the new entrant student number is 2,163,682 with 1,875,337 students being admitted at academic HEIs and 176,022 others at vocational HEIs or diploma programs. Education field is the most favorite study program for new students applying to academic institutions with a total of 435,986 new entrants. Meanwhile, various fields of study in engineering have attracted58.130 new entrants at vocational institutions. In terms of higher educational degree being enrolled into, as many as 7,094,081 (95.16%)students attend undergraduate level, 316,615 (4.25%) students at master's degree, and the remaining 43,883 (0,59%) are doctorate students. The average ages of undergraduate students are 18-30 years old, master students 25-40 years old, and doctorate students 40-50 years old.

By 2020, the number of faculty members or lecturers of HEIs in Indonesia has reached 312,890 persons. In terms of educational qualification, the majority of Indonesian lecturers hold Master's degree (207, 586), followed by Doctorate degree (42,825) and Bachelor degree (30,612). The rest number of faculties consists of personnel with various educational qualification background ranging from 4-year-diploma program, specialist, to professional certification.

In assuring the eligibility in providing education at tertiary level, each established HEI in Indonesia must undergo an assessment of national accreditation. This accreditation procedure is one of the government efforts in maintaining the nationwide HEIs quality standard. The higher education institution accreditation criteria are based on the assessment for the eligibility after which an institution can be classified as *A, B, C, Excellent, Very Good, Good,* and *Not Yet Accredited* (Directorate General of Higher Education, 2020). The national accreditation board of Indonesian higher education is conducted by either one of two bodies. The first is Higher Education National Accreditation Body (*Badan Akreditasi Nasional Perguruan Tinggi [BANPT]*) which is administered by the central government under the MoEC, and the second is Non-government/independent Accreditation Body of Higher Education (*Lembaga Akreditasi Mandiri Perguruan Tinggi [LAMPT]*) which is organized by any relevant associations of study program such as in health disciplines with its *Non-government/independent Accreditation Body of Higher Education in Health (LAMPTKes)*. In addition, while working on improving the quality of higher education domestically, since 2015, Indonesia is among a few developing countries who are making their effort to send some of their best universities to be recognized as a World Class University (WCU) and to achieve global reputation.

The internationalization initiation has also been reflected in the government's concern on encouraging the universities and study programs to seek international accreditation provided by foreign accreditation agencies or those which are internationally recognized. As guidelines, in January 2020, the Indonesian Ministry of Education and Culture (MoEC) issued a Ministerial Decree No. 83/P/2020 announcing the list of 22 International Accreditation Agencies than can be used as a reference for Indonesian HEIs. Later in the same year, in August 2020, the MoEC announced additional 18 international accreditation agencies to the list in the Ministerial Decree of MoEC No. 754/P/2020 regulating the Main Indicators of Public Higher Education Institutions. Up to the date of this study, the best universities in Indonesia have been dominated by public universities. This explains the reason behind the appointment of top eleven public universities to participate in Indonesian National World Class University Program 2015-2019. The best universities in Indonesia are dominated by public universities.

3. Methods

This research is a case study examining how eleven selected public higher education institutions in Indonesia have performed in taking part in World Class University (WCU) program initiated by Indonesian government as mandated in the decree of Indonesian MoRTHE No. 50 year 2017. The eleven HEIs are Universitas Gadjah Mada (UGM), Universitas Indonesia (UI), Institut Teknologi Bandung (ITB), Universitas Airlangga (Unair), Institut Pertanian Bogor (IPB), Institut Teknologi Sepuluh November (ITS), Universitas Padjajaran (Unpad), Universitas Diponegoro (Undip), Universitas Brawijaya (UB), Universitas Hasanuddin (Unhas), and Universitas Sebelas Maret (UNS). More specifically, this study focuses on the impact of the trend in research, publication, and collaboration of Indonesian higher education institutions (HEIs) on their world university ranking and the implications of the potential challenges and opportunities have on Indonesian HEIs. This research is limited on investigating the program outputs and the trend of the data collected within the timeframe of the first batch of Indonesian WCU program from 2015 to 2019.

Three sources that had been identified as relevant in providing the data for this study consist of the *SciVal* database (https://www.scival.com), the Quacquarelli Symonds World University Rankings (QS WUR) (https://www.topuniversities.com/qs-world-university-rankings), and Indonesian Directorate of Higher Education database (https://pddikti.kemdikbud.go.id).

The *SciVal* is online analytical tool developed by Elsevier that provides research data derived from Scopus and ScienceDirect. The *SciVal* has recorded data on research performance of more than 20,700 research institution along with their worldwide associated researchers from 234 nations. The *SciVal* also allows analysis of the data from Scopus database that covers more than 55 million publication records from over 22,000 international journals (https://www.scival.com).

The Quacquarelli Symonds World University Rankings (QS WUR) database provides tables featuring 1,300 universities worldwide. Each university's ranking are based on six key metrics of Academic Reputation (40%), Employer Reputation (10%), Faculty/Student Ratio (20%), Citations per faculty (20%), International Faculty Ratio (5%), and International Student Ratio (5%) (https://www.topuniversities.com/qs-world-university-rankings/methodology). Lastly, the Indonesian Directorate of Higher Education database named *Pangkalan Data Pendidikan Tinggi (PDDikti)* is a national database that provide any relevant statistical data on Indonesian higher education institutions information and it is accessible at https://pddikti.kemdikbud.go.id.

In addition to evaluating the whole performance of eleven universities selected to participate in Indonesian national WCU Program, specific highlights and exposures to be given to three prominent institutions, Universitas Gadjah Mada (UGM), Universitas Indonesia (UI), and Institut Teknologi Bandung (ITB), that have achieved Indonesian WCU program's goal by being successfully enlisted in the Top 500 QS WUR. Furthermore, data from QS WUR Top 500 universities in Southeast Asia were also presented to compare their achievement in QS WUR.

The collected data were analyzed descriptively by showing trend analysis, comparative analysis, and WUR indicator analysis to see how each university has met the required criteria. Specific analysis was done in the aspect of academic or scholarly publication and collaboration as these two, based on the reviewed previous studies, were considered by the writers as the strongest predictors for WUR. By so doing, it is expected to provide a brief framework for further studies that are more comprehensive in analyzing the performance of the universities by considering strengths, weaknesses, opportunities, and threats that each university should address as they have already been granted more autonomy as public universities with legal entity or in Indonesian HEI system, it is called as *PTNBH* (*Perguruan Tinggi Negeri Badan Hukum* [Legal Entity State University])

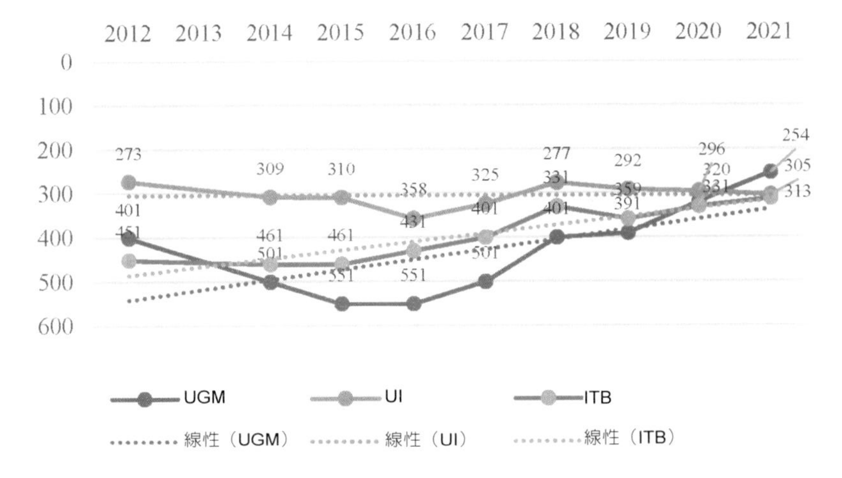

Figure 1 Trend of 3 Indonesian Universities in Top 500 WUR

Note. Trend of 3 Top 500 WUR of Indonesian Universities. From Top 500 Global WUR Target.

4. Findings and Discussion

4.1. The Impact of the Research, Publication, and Collaboration of Indonesia HEIs on Their World University Ranking

4.1.1. Top 500 WUR Achievement of Indonesian HEIs

As stated in the 2015-2019 strategic planning of MoRTHE, five universities were targeted to be enlisted on the Top 500 WUR by 2019. However, only three institutions have achieved the targets. The three institutions are Universitas Gadjah Mada (UGM), Universitas Indonesia (UI), and Institut Teknologi Bandung (ITB)ranked 254, 305, and 313 respectively. These three have been well-known for their reputation in Indonesia as the top three universities. Since

Table 2 Indicators of WUR of Indonesian 3 Top 500 from 2018 – 2021

Univ	Rank	Year	Overall Score	Academic Reputation	Employer Reputation	Faculty Student Ration	International Faculty	International Students	Citations Per Faculty
UGM	254	2018	-	48.8	42.2	-	23.5	-	-
		2019	28.6	37.4	36	38.5	36.5	2.6	1.5
		2020	33.2	41.3	36.7	51.3	42.9	2.5	1.6
		2021	37.4	44.9	43.2	59.9	48.7	2.2	1.7
UI	305	2018	39.2	48.1	60.1	44.3	87.1	-	
		2019	34.8	36.1	51.3	49.1	93.9	5.5	1.8
		2020	34.7	39.5	47.3	43.4	94.5	5	1.9
		2021	34	40.9	52.9	35.9	88.3	3.4	2.1
ITB	313	2018	35.3	52.9	56.1	31	30.1	-	
		2019	30.4	36.2	41.7	43.9	42.1	2.6	3.2
		2020	32.3	39.3	39.8	51.3	29.2	1.6	3.7
		2021	33.3	38.3	45.1	52.8	36.3	1.7	4

Note. Indicators of WUR of Indonesian 3 Top 500 from 2018 – 2021. From Top 500 Global WUR Target.

2013, they have already been in the Top 500 WUR although UI once was the highest among the three, but then fell into the second in the most recent QS WUR 2021 list. Here is the trend of their WUR from 2013 to 2021.

Overall, the trend seems to be increasing among these three universities, but as the WCU project of MoRTHE targeted five universities to sit in the highest 500 worldwide, the increase does not look promising. In addition, looking at the development or trend from 2018 to 2021 indicator assessment, it is clear that UGM has outperformed the other two universities significantly during the last period of year. Here is the detailed indicator improvement as shown in Table 2.

Compared to UI, UGM performed better in the academic reputation and faculty-student ratio, while in the employer reputation, international faculty, international students and citations per faculty, UGM still lags behind UI. ITB, however, still remains at the third rank among the three in the Top 500 WUR.

4.1.2. Indonesian HEIs Research and Publication

This study focuses on the efforts done by the HEIs in Indonesia to achieve world-class university ranking by being in the Top 500 universities in WUR. Emphasis is given in the research and its output to support HEI reputation. From the Accountability Report of MoRTHE 2019, research and publications targets have been mostly achieved as shown in Table 3.

Table 3 The Achievement of Research and Publications Targets by 2019

No.	Programs	Target	Achievement	
			Number	%
1	Number of Mature Science and Technology Park	22	22	100
2	Science and Technology Centre	90	103	114.44
3	International Publication	72,237	97,057	134
4	Registered Innovative Products	9,000	10,435	115.94

No.	Programs	Target	Achievement	
			Number	%
5	R&D Prototype	4,045	5,802	143.43
6	Industrial Prototype	120	246	205
7	Innovation Products	190	236	124

Note. The Achievement of Research and Publications Targets by 2019. From Accountability Report of MoRTHE 2019.

In addition, it is revealed that both national and institutional indicators have been achieved. The improving number of Indonesian HEIs that are accredited A by the BAN-PT indicates that the institutional quality of Indonesian universities is increasing as shown in the following table.

Table 4 The Number of HEIs Accredited A by Indonesian BAN-PT in 2015-2019

Year	Number Targeted	Number Achieved
2015	29	26
2016	39	49
2017	59	65
2018	80	85
2019	110	96
2015-2019	110	96 (87.27%)

Note. The Number of HEIs Accredited A by Indonesian BAN-PT in 2015-2019. From Accountability Report 2019 MoRTHE.

In addition, the number of study programs across Indonesian HEIs that had been accredited *B* by BAN-PT also increased from 11,617 in 2018 into 12,371 in 2019 which also indicates its target achievement for *B* accreditation set at 68.40% to be overachieved by 69.05%. Below is the detailed achievement of the national and international accreditation status of HEIs in 2020 based on the types of HEIs.

Table 5 Indonesian National and International HEIs Accreditation Achievement 2020

Type of HEIs	National Accreditation(%)			International Accreditation(%)
	A	B	C	
Public	37.43	39.96	4.72	9.27
Ministerial/government	19.90	44.81	4.71	NA
Private	6.91	46.38	21.45	NA
Religious	7.16	28.87	25.79	NA

Note. Indonesian National and International HEIs Accreditation Achievement in 2020. From Accountability Report of Director of Higher Education of MoEC, 2020.

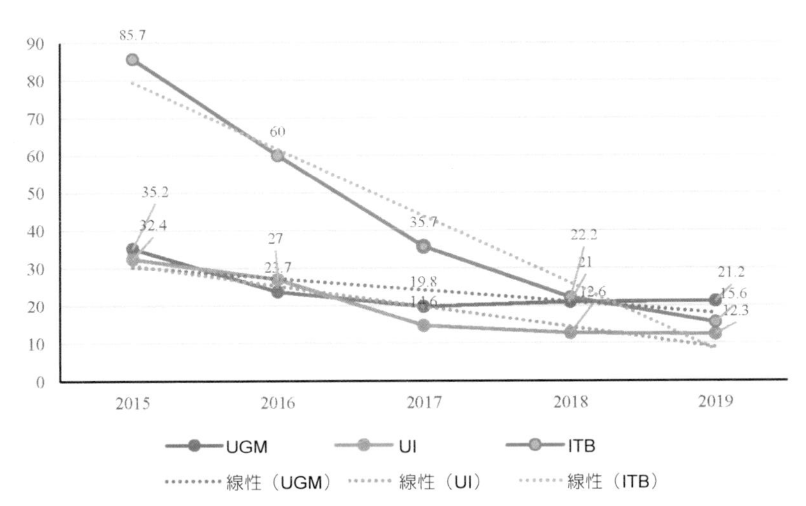

Figure 3 International Collaboration (%) of 3 Top 500 Universities in Indonesia.

Note. International Collaboration of 3 Top 500 Universities in Indonesia. From SciVal datasets 2015-2019.

4.1.3. Indonesian HEIs' International Collaboration for Increasing Research Performance

Specifically, this paper aims to evaluate the academic performance of the universities by focusing on the publication performance. Based on the data from SciVal, there is an implication that these universities have made some strategies dealing with improving their performance in publication as can be seen in the following Figure.

There is a decreasing trend in the collaborations that have been conducted by the universities from 2015 until 2019. However, the decreasing collaborations do not impact on the decreasing performance in their publications as shown in the figure below.

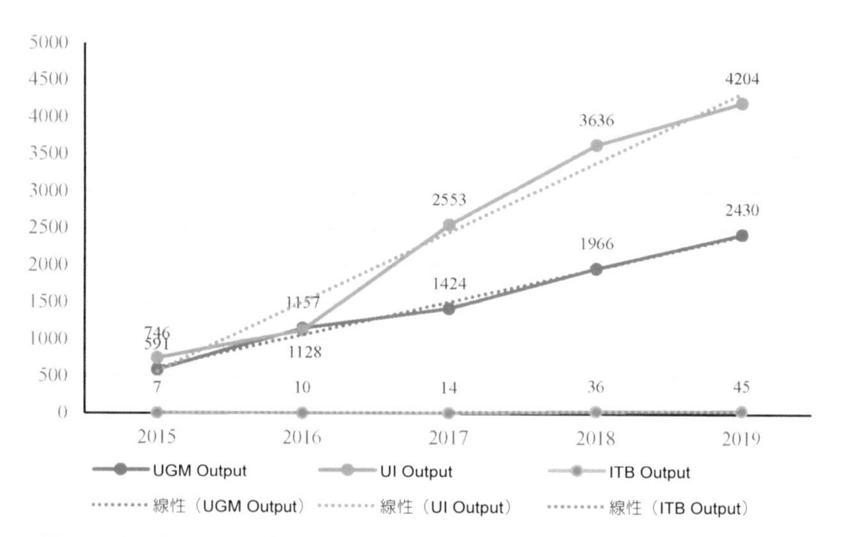

Figure 4 Scholarly Output Increase of 3 Top 500 WUR of Indonesian Universities

Note. Scholarly Output Increase of 3 Top 500 WUR of Indonesian Universities. From SciVal datasets 2015-2019.

The graphic of Figure 4 indicates that the universities' publications even show significant increase from 2015 to 2019. This is also in line with the Accountability Report of MoRTHE about the increasing number of

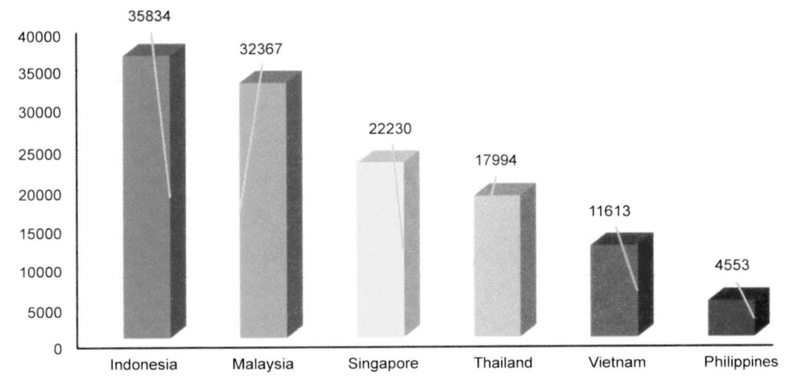

Figure 5 Comparison of Scholarly Publications among Countries in Southeast Asia

Note. Comparison of Scholarly Publications among Countries in South East Asia. From Accountability Report 2019 MoRTHE.

international publications of Indonesian universities, which exceed other countries in South East Asian as presented in the following figure.

Based on the data, this achievement is more than the target set for 2019 by MoRTHE, that is 35,000 international publications, or 102.38% of the performance indicator achievement. In addition, from 72,237 international publications targeted from 2015 - 2019, a total of 97,056 were resulted, thus accounting for 134.36% achievement of the performance indicator.

However, it should be noted that even though increasing in their publication number, the citations of the publications do not show a linear increase as their citations. Also, although Indonesian position in Scientific Journal Ranking (SJR) in 2019 increased 4 levels into 48 with H-Index of 214, compared to that in 2018 in the 52nd with H-Index of 196, compared to the other ASEAN countries, Indonesian position is just above Vietnam and the Philippines. Moreover, this was also shown from the SciVal website that the numbers of citations were going down as shown in the following figure.

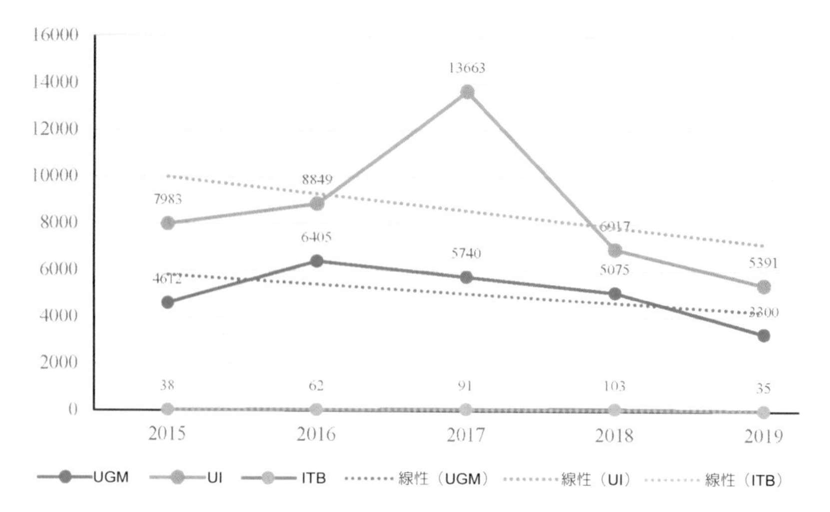

Figure 6　Citation Trend from 2015 to 2019 of Top 500 WUR of Indonesian Universities

Note. Citation Trend from 2015 to 2019 of Top 500 WUR of Indonesian Universities. From SciVal datasets 2015-2019.

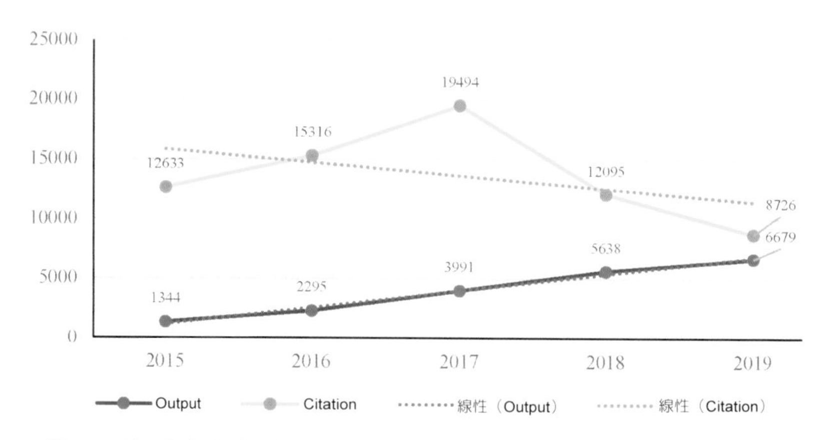

Figure 7　Scholarly Publication Compared to Citations of 3 Top 500 WUR of Indonesian Universities

Note. Scholarly Publication Compared to Citations of 3 Top 500 WUR of Indonesian Universities. From SciVal datasets 2015-2019.

Table 6 Comparison of Top 500 Universities in South East Asia

# Rank	University	Overall Score	Academic Reputation	Employer Reputation	Faculty Student Ratio	Int. Faculty	Int. Students	Citations/ Faculty	Country
11	National University of Singapore (NUS)	91.5	99.7	98.4	90.7	100	71.4	72.9	SIN
13	Nanyang Technological University, Singapore (NTU)	89.9	89.8	89.8	91.5	100	67.6	89	SIN
59	Universiti Malaya (UM)	70.1	74.1	84.6	82.1	68.7	44.5	47.7	MAS
132	Universiti Putra Malaysia (UPM)	52.7	50.5	52.8	76.1	58.1	86.5	22.3	MAS
141	Universiti Kebangsaan Malaysia (UKM)	52	53.8	55.7	93.3	31.2	40.8	11.9	MAS
142	Universiti Sains Malaysia (USM)	51.9	56	60.5	76.2	37.6	49.9	17.6	MAS
187	Universiti Teknologi Malaysia	44.2	39.4	51.6	64.4	27.6	63.9	27.8	MAS
208	Chulalongkorn University	41.6	67.1	60.7	29.1	14.6	2.6	9	THA
252	Mahidol University	37.5	41.7	44.4	69.6	8.6	5.6	7.8	THA
254	Gadjah Mada University	37.4	44.9	43.2	59.9	48.7	2.2	1.7	INA
254	Universiti Brunei Darussalam (UBD)	37.4	18.3	10.5	95.4	100	63.9	7.9	BRU
305	Universitas Indonesia	34	40.9	52.9	35.9	88.3	3.4	2.1	INA

# Rank	University	Overall Score	Academic Reputation	Employer Reputation	Faculty Student Ratio	Int. Faculty	Int. Students	Citations/ Faculty	Country
313	Bandung Institute of Technology (ITB)	33.3	38.3	45.1	52.8	36.3	1.7	4	INA
350	Universiti Teknologi Brunei	30.9	11.5	9.1	91.5	99.3	7.6	7.8	BRU
379	Taylor's University	28.9	16.4	60.7	41.3	52	86.1	4.5	MAS
391	UCSI University	28.5	15.1	44.7	55.2	37	81.3	4.4	MAS
396	University of the Philippines	28.2	34.1	40.8	48.4	1.4	1.4	2.4	PHI
439	Universiti Teknologi PETRONAS (UTP)	26	15	29.8	32.5	83	22.5	25.6	MAS

Note. Comparison of Top 500 Universities in South East Asia. From Top 500 Global WUR Target.

The comparison between the scholarly output and citation is shown in Figure 7.

4.1.4. Comparison between Indonesian HEIs and those in South East Asian Countries

It is necessary to see how Indonesian universities have progressed in comparison to those from other countries in the neighboring countries, specifically in south east Asian countries. It is important to measure how Indonesian universities can compete with the others in the same region seeing that the government has funded them for WCU project aimed at increasing their reputation, which indirectly also increasing their reputation compared to the other participating universities. Here is the comparison of those in the Top 500 WUR among universities in South East Asian countries.

Although only three Indonesian universities sit on the Top 500 WUR in 2020, there is an optimism that in the near future, there will be more Indonesian universities can position themselves in the elite group as currently five universities have already been in the Top 1000 QS WUR 2021. The five universities and their rankings are Airlangga University (521-530), Bogor Agricultural University (531-540), Institute Technology Sepuluh Nopember (751-800), Bina Nusantara University (801-1000), and Universitas Padjajaran (801-1000).

4.2. The Implications of the Potential Challenges and Opportunities on Indonesian HEIs in Achieving the National Goals for Internationalization (WCU Program)

As previously stated, this paper is intended to describe how Indonesian HEIs' efforts towards internationalization have shown good progress in the achievement of domestic target or goals but, when compared to other countries in the internationalization, Indonesia has to strive more in order to catch up with the competing HEIs in the neighboring countries, especially among ASEAN countries. The performance indicator in Top 500 WCU ranking has not successfully met yet as by the end of 2020 only three instead of five universities are listed in the Top 500 of the QS WUR. The three universities are Universitas Gadjah Mada (UGM), Universitas Indonesia (UI), and Institut Teknologi Bandung (ITB). The result indicates that although the national WCU program goal has not yet accomplished fully, both Indonesian government and HEIs managements have work harder to get very close to meet the set target.

In terms of WUR, Indonesian universities still need to work very hard to catch up with other neighboring countries, especially Malaysia in getting into the Top 500 universities. Among 4,620 universities in Indonesia, only three are in the top 500 or only 11 are in the Top 1000 WUR, compared to Malaysia that can place 8 universities in the Top 500 WUR with only 590 universities. This low achievement of Indonesia in the Top 500 WUR can be due to some factors as follows: (1) lack of commitment from the HEIs to increase their WUR,(2) lack of reliable funding sources (the main funding source for WCU of each university still very much dependent on Central Government),(3) low lecturer/student ratio,(4) low indexed published journal articles and citation index,(5) low number of foreign students,(6), poor database system to support policy making, and(7) low networking with global stakeholders and universities (DGHE Accountability Report, 2019).

Among the 11 universities targeted to reach Top 500 WUR, only three have achieved the targets, others are still quite far behind, thus requiring more efforts to do under new department, as the ministry is not any more MoRTHE, but Ministry of Education and Culture, and Higher education is now under the Directorate General office which institutionally is not as strong as the previous ministry. This raises skepticism even, as planning and funding will be much dependent on the other directorate general, such as elementary and middle school education. However, there is still a hope for better university ranking as more universities have been granted more autonomy through what is called PTNBH (*Perguruan Tinggi Negeri Badan Hukum* [Legal Entity State University]) in which planning, budgeting, staffing, and academic policy are more autonomous compared to that the universities with lower status of PTNBLU (*Perguruan Tinggi Negeri Badan Layanan Umum* [Public Service State University]) and PTN Satker (*Perguruan Tinggi Negeri Satuan Kerja* [Working Unit State University]).

Based on the findings on both the challenges and the performances of Indonesian universities within national and institutional levels, Indonesian government could consider several strategies to boost the institutional performance of its top universities to be enlisted in the Top 500 global WUR and to keep advancing in the list for those universities already enlisted at the Top 300-400. The government should, however set a more realistic expectation made in line with the universities and government capacities in creating WCUs. Referring back to the conceptual frameworks on establishing WCU proposed by Lee (2013), it would be beneficial for Indonesian government to adopt (1) realistic expectation,(2) differentiated educational system,(3) improving quality of higher education system,(4) selection of target fields and global partnership, and(5) enabling governance.

As to 2020, Indonesian higher education (HE) system has not differentiated HEIs into research versus comprehensive or teaching university yet. Most HEIs are either comprehensive or vocational. However, Indonesian MoEC seems to start addressing this issue as being written in their document of Strategic Plan 2020-2024 mentioning the need for the differentiation of HEIs to have each institution focus to be a research university, teaching university, or vocational university. Also, considering the vast number of HEIs in Indonesia, it must be reasonable not to target all of them to become WCUs in simultaneous time. Thus, the MoEC's strategic plan to establish *Science Techno Park* at five top public universities, Universitas Gadjah Mada (UGM), University of Indonesia (UI), Institute of Technology Bandung (ITB), Institut Pertanian Bogor (IPB), and Institut Teknologi Sepuluh Nopember (ITS)can be a prominent starting point in HEI differentiation model by mandating these five universities to be the first Indonesian research universities. The shifting of focus from comprehensive to research university can be an appropriate strategy to have more universities at the Top 500 list considering that most of those seen at the WUR top list are research universities. The next strategies of improving quality of higher education system and enabling governance should come side by side, too. National policy needs to be as favorable as possible to the improvement of HEIs system and governance quality, while at the same time has the supervisory and control functions. Lastly, considering that the ranking decision made by any WUR system is more normative assessment, meaning that the position of a university in the WUR list is always relative to the performance of other competition universities, the selection of target fields and global partnership is definitely crucial. Therefore, planning strategic collaborations with other world class universities that are at the top list of global WUR should be prioritized. The bright side for Indonesian HEIs is that, Indonesian MoEC's Strategic Plan 2020-2024 explicitly states the plan to improve the collaboration and cooperation with international word class universities listed at the top 100 of QS and/or THE WUR. Besides, the collaboration with other prominent national, regional, or international research institutions and industries, must be encouraged, too. When the strategies are matched and made compatible with the available resources at both national level and institutional level of individual university, working together to reach the national goal of WCU project in Indonesia must be seen feasible and reachable.

However, International publications have increased very significantly as the MoRTHE has targeted higher publications by empowering all potential lecturers and postgraduate students to publish internationally. Postgraduate students are required to publish in Scopus indexed journals for their graduation requirement as stipulated in the decree of Indonesian MoRTHE or *Permenristekdikti* No 54/2015 about National Standard for Indonesian Higher Education. In addition, more incentives have been offered for the faculties if they publish in international Scopus indexed journals. This is supported by having more collaborations with reputable universities in joint research and publications to boost the number of publications of Indonesian scholars. These strategies are considered effective so far in terms of increasing the quantity, but in terms of the quality, as measured by citation index, Indonesia still lags behind other countries, such as Singapore, Malaysia, Thailand, only higher than Vietnam and the Philippines. This indicates that other countries also are working very hard to increase their publication and citation index, and they have strategies for better citations.

5. Conclusion

University reputation can be used to measure how educational quality of a country has been performed in comparison to other countries. Every country has been devoting its potential to boost HEI internationalization, indicated by the WUR, so that it will give more impact to marketization and better human resource quality. Indonesian universities, despite their high number compared to those in the regional area, still place three of them in the Top 500

WUR table. The MoRTHE program called WCU Project still seems not quite successful as indicated by only three universities in the list. However, this can be due to the increasing position of other universities worldwide that are also working to achieve the elite position in the WUR. This challenging situation can actually be treated as an opportunity through careful design of both policies and strategies that regulate and focus on improving both the quantity and quality of institutional and individual collaborations between Indonesian HEIs and their faculty members with other countries' reputable HEIs and university faculties. Also, when the WUR position is set as a target, putting the results of this study under the scenario of the methodological framework and the metrics scoring of the targeted WUR should be beneficial in finding appropriate strategies for earning more scores resulting in more advancing level in the WUR.

For example, the problem faced by the participating HEIs, even those among the national top public universities, in gaining the goal of Indonesian government's WCU program seems to refer back to the Figure 3 and 4 in the findings of this study showing that although the declining number or collaboration do not have impact on the Indonesian faculty members' publication performance within the 2015-2019-time frame, the citation number, however, shows as continuously decreasing as indicated by Figure 6 and 7. This kind of empirical data can be used as a valuable materials in provisioning effective and efficient plans to deal with the lower scores of the most significant indicators in the QS top universities global ranking that contribute significantly to the total scores i.e. Academic Reputation (40%) and Citation per Faculty (20%). Considering the nature of the methodology used to determine the Academic Reputation score in the QS WUR which is done through survey distributed to academics worldwide asking them to nominate up to 10 domestic and up to thirty international higher education institutions by excluding their own institutions (https://www.topuniversities.com/qs-world-university-rankings/methodology), a given university needs to identify an in-point strategy to gain more listing by the respondents. For instance, improving the quantity of collaboration with reputable faculties or academics and other higher education institutions must then be able to facilitate this aforementioned interest, making it more convenient in contacting and nominating potential respondents yielding on more reliable results on Academic Reputation scoring. Further studies generating more empirical data is then also needed in order to detect the aspects of collaboration that will contribute highly in promoting the citation numbers like the position of the partner universities in WUR, the reputation of the academics and researchers, the field of disciplines, and the intensity and sparing roles in collaboration.

Considering that the efforts of improving both the quantity and the quality of WCU in Indonesia belongs to government's initiation, the results of this study may bring implication on government policy in further managing the national WCU program, so that the participating universities have access to clearer guidelines made as the basis for planning executable strategies to achieve the goal. This matter is very crucial because the national WCU program comes with the expectation of not only refining the quality and achieving the higher reputation of the country's HEIs but also to have significant impact for Indonesia as a country to compete in a more globalized world through its higher education sector. Therefore, based on the results gained at the end of the program in 2019, Indonesian government through its Directorate General of Higher Education (DGHE) has issued a policy addressing the WUR of Indonesian HEIs.

This study has provided an overview of the performance of higher education institutions in Indonesia, especially the reputable ones, in enhancing their research, publication, and collaboration in order to keep up with the internationalization, specifically in upgrading their WUR, as supported by the MoRTHE though the WCU programs. The findings can be the bases for the MoRTHE and the universities to evaluate their policy as stated in their strategic planning and see whether the key performance indicator (KPI) should be adjusted based on the dynamics of higher education institutions in the regional and international contexts. This study can also provide a different perspective of how worldwide university ranking and databases measure the effectiveness of WUR program with objective measures.

Although more hard work is still needed, the Internationalization has provided the opportunities for Indonesian HEIs to (1) excel in their academic programs by improving the teaching and learning, research, and community service quality along with improved academic and non-academic facilities, supported by more productive international collaboration,(2) improve economic benefits by increasing the number of international students studying in Indonesia, and (3) strengthen more social impacts as quality universities will produce more innovations and models for society empowerment to uplift poverty and increase life quality of the Indonesian people. More efforts and commitment need to be done in the coming years, but as some HEIs are approaching the top 500 positions, there is an opportunity to reach Top 500.

Some strategies can be considered in order to uplift the reputations of Indonesian universities:(1) upgrading the qualification of human resources through education by setting up a minimum of doctoral degree for lecturers,(2) providing more support for research and publication by providing more funding and infrastructure to answer the needs of advanced research outputs for higher publication citation, and (3) reformulating the policy of lecturer load in conducting the main tasks of teaching, research, and community service to be more oriented towards improved academic reputation internationally. More studies however should be conducted by using qualitative measures to have deeper analysis by involving policy makers, lecturers, and other stakeholders to address the factors that have hindered the productivity of research and how university reputation can be uplifted in response to the tighter HE internationalization.

References

Alimi, M.Y., & Rokhman, F. (2017). Leap strategies to increase international publication of Indonesian higher education: an example of Semarang State University. *The Social Sciences, 12* (7), 1299-1304. doi:10.36478/sscience.2017.1299.1304

Altbach, P. G. (2004). The costs and benefits of world-class universities. *Academe, 90*(1), 20-23. doi:10.2307/40252583

Cartes-Velásquez, R., & Manterola, C. (2017). Impact of collaboration on research quality: A case analysis of dental research. *International Journal of Information Science and Management, 15*(1), 89-93.

Ceballos, H. G., Fangmeyer Jr, J., Galeano, N., Juarez, E., & Cantu-Ortiz, F. J. (2017). Impelling research productivity and impact through collaboration: A scientometric case study of knowledge management. *Knowledge Management Research and Practice*, 346-355.

Darmadji, A., Prasojo, L.D., Kusumaningrum, F.A., & Andriansyah, Y. (2018). Research productivity and international collaboration of top Indonesian universities. *Current Science, 115*(4), 653-658.

Dewi, A. U. (2018). Towards Knowledge Economy: A Comparative Study of Indonesian and South Korean Internationalization of Higher Education. *Knowledge and Social Transformation*, 63-83.

Fu, YC., Baker, D.P. & Zhang, L. (2020). Engineering a world class university? The impact of Taiwan' s world class university project on scientific productivity. *Higher Education Policy, 33*, 555–570. doi:10.1057/s41307-018-0110-z

Hazelkorn, Ellen. (2011). Measuring world- class excellence and the global obsession with rankings in King, R., Marginson, S., and Naidoo, R. (Eds). *Handbook on Globalization and Higher Education*. Pages 497-515. Glos: Edward Elgar Publishing Limited.

Jarvis, D. S., & Mok, K. H. (2019). *Transformations in higher education governance in Asia: Policy, politics and progress.* Singapore: Springer Nature.

Lee, J. (2013). Creating world-class universities: Implications for developing countries. *PROSPECTS, 43*(2), 233–249. doi:10.1007/s11125-013-9266-x

Liu, N.C., Wang, Q., & Cheng, Y. (2011). *Paths to a world-class university: Lessons from practices and experiences.* Rotterdam: Sense Publishers.

Lo, W. Y. W., & Hou, A. Y. C. (2019). A farewell to internationalisation? Striking a balance between global ambition and local needs in higher education in Taiwan. *Higher Education, 80,* 497–510. https://doi.org/10.1007/s10734-019-00495-0

Macaro, E., Curle, S., Pun, J., An, J., & Dearden, J. (2017). *A systematic review of English medium instruction in higher education. Language Teaching, 51(01), 36–76.* doi:10.1017/s0261444817000350

Ministry of Education and Culture. (2020). *Rencana Strategis Kementrian Pendidikan dan Kebudayaan 2020-2024.* Jakarta: Kemendikbud Indonesia.

Ministry of Research, Technology, and Higher Education. (2017). *Peraturan Menteri Riset, Teknologi, dan Pendidikan Tinggi Republik Indonesia No. 50 Tahun 2017 tentang Rencana Strategis Kementerian Riset, Teknologi, dan Pendidikan Tinggi Tahun 2015-2019.* Jakarta: Kemenristekdikti Indonesia.

Mok, K. H. (2011). Regional responses to globalization challenges: The assertion of soft power and changing university governance in Singapore, Hong Kong and Malaysia. In R. King, S. Marginson & R. Naidoo, *Handbook on Globalization and Higher Education* (pp. 180-196). Massachuset: Edward Elgar Publishing Inc.

Nandiyanto, ABD, Biddinika, M.K., & Triawan, F. (2020). How bibliographic dataset portrays decreasing number of scientific publication from Indonesia. *Indonesian Journal of Science & Technology, 5* (1), 154-175. doi:10.17509/ijost.v5i1.22265

N.K., S., Mathew K., S. & Cherukodan, S. (2018). Impact of scholarly output on University Ranking. *Global Knowledge, Memory and Communication, 67*(3), 154-165. doi:10.1108/GKMC-11-2017-0087

Secretariat Directorate General of Higher Education. (2020). Higher Education Statistical Year Book 2020. Jakarta: Secretariat Directorate General of Higher Education, MoEC.

Shin, J.C., & Kehm, B.M. (Eds). (2013). *Institutionalization of World-Class University in global competition*. Dordrecht: Springer.

Zhou, P., & Cai, X. (2018). Funding, collaboration and research performance: A comparative study of leading universities in China and the USA. *STI 2018 Conference Proceedings: Proceedings of the 23rd International Conference on Science and Technology Indicators*. Leiden: Centre for Science and technology Studies (CWTS) Leiden University.

探討教學創新對職場能力之啟發效益

國立東華大學資訊管理學系兼校務研究辦公室行政支援組
侯佳利、謝坤霖

國立東華大學校務研究辦公室
吳佳燕

壹、當教學遇上創新

創新是當代社會與經濟發展的重要議題，國際組織「經濟合作暨發展組織（Organization for Economic Cooperation and Development，OECD）」將創新定義為「不同於過去的嶄新且進步的產品或流程」（OECD/Eurosta, 2018, p. 20）。在教育領域，創新可有四種重要應用，1. 將創新產品視為嶄新的教材如課綱、教科書、或學習資源。2. 新流程則可視為知識服務的傳輸方式如數位學習。3. 新的組織活動，例如透過數位科技與學生或其家人的溝通方式。4. 新的市場技術，例如高階研究所層級的課程差異化定價（Vincent-Lancrin et al., 2017）。

美國教育部將創新視為使用非傳統方法的教學計畫，包括數位媒體和工具的應用等等，來加強學生的學習效果，並每年專案投入逾億美元的預算，支持教學創新在基礎教育的推動（U. S. Department of Education, 2016）。根據Education Week（2018）的調查，超過半數的教師認為創新是學校或地區下一階段的優先事項。

創新概念應普及至各級教育機構（Halász, 2018），在高教領域，教學創新的概念同樣日趨重要，教學創新著重的不單是傳送知識，還必須重視學生如何運用知識（Papaleontiou-Louca et al., 2014），以及透過課程設計與規劃來增進學生應付未來環境的能力（Tassone et al., 2018）。近年在台灣，相關政策的大力推動支持為教學創新的發展注入不少能量，如106年的「教學創新先導計畫」與107年啟動的「高等教育深耕計畫」，均希望以學生為主體，由校方與教師規劃更能培育學生多向能力的課程。

教學創新的實際執行過程，例如「翻轉教室」的概念，能夠從學習時間、師生角色、學習結果等方面都展現異於傳統教學的模式（羅寶鳳，2016）。尤其現今科技進步，對實踐教學創新提供充分的條件，如多媒體的評量與教學溝通就很方便教師運用教材以及收集學習資料，讓教師設計創新的教案更有助益（林志成，2016）。加上線上教學平臺與教學影片盛行，可用來強化學生自主學習、共同學習、成果分享的過程，讓學生用自己習慣的方式，依照學習進度不同來修習艱深的專業課程（郭廸賢、陳羿薰，2019）。基此，本研究與上述提及的教學創新概念有相同的看法，並將教學創新視為是培育大學生多向能力的智能教學方式（Uskov et al., 2018）。而以創新（innovation）、創意（creativity）、創業（entrepreneurship）之思維為主體的三創課程即是體現教學創新的方式之一（楊文華、莊姍姍、李宗政，2011）。

貳、共通職能培育

在大學裡的教學創新，教師透過教學方法、課程內容、評量設計、教學工具、數位科技等等，發展不同於傳統的教學方法以及應用在課程之中。教學理念與方法構成後，勢必需要思量教學的成果，即學生可能學習到什麼？

不少教學創新的研究聚焦於將傳統課堂調整為適合培育開放風氣與學習動力的教育環境（Cremin, 2009; Soh, 2000, 2015; Sharma & Sharma, 2018; Dikici, 2013; Kandemir et al., 2019）。這些研究常用於中小學教育環境，但在大學中實行的教學創新過程，需考量高教的獨特性，一者大學本為一開放學習的環境，學涯裡會修習的課程種類繁多，所謂「教室環境」隨課程和學系經常變化，難以一概而論。二者學生身處社會和校園生活的中介點，這使得人們更加關注知識涵養與就業發展的雙重需求。

根據勞動部勞動力發展署的「台灣就業通」（2019）調查顯示，雇用方錄用社會新鮮人時重視「相關實習經驗與打工經驗」、「專業知識與技術」。而新鮮人職場主要優勢依序為「於對新事物接受度高」、「對新興科技、網路資訊的掌握度高」、「可塑性較高」、「學習能力強」、「創造力強」。可見得就業過程中，於爭取錄取的階段會注重專業職能，而職場上的發展可能更需要共通職能中的特質。

台灣近年來已有大學生共通職能之概念應用，如教育部2009年開始推動的「大專校院就業職能平台」（University Career and Competency Assessment Network，簡稱UCAN）深具代表性，UCAN平台目前為國內眾多大學使用的職能探索資源，本研究即採用其八項職場共通職能：溝通表達、持續學習、人際互動、團隊合作、問題解決、創新、工作責任與紀律、資訊科技應用作為職能探討。這些能力為經由跨域專家共同討論並經過統計科學鑑定，所設計出符合我國環境的職能項目，其內涵為進入各類職場都需具備的能力（楊玉惠，2013）。

職能教育和教學創新的構想應有整合之處，職能教育的課程規劃，注重以學生為核心多於教師為核心，讓實作與學習並進（Wesselink et al.,2007; Mulder et al., 2009），而教學創新課程的目標，經常是希望培養學生多項能力的整合，譬如盧以琳與黃鼎倫（2018）透過創新教學的實驗課程強化學生在問題解決、跨域整合、基礎通識能力、科技資訊、創新創業等能力。鄭夙珍與鄭瀛川（2014）針對心理系學生從課程引導溝通表達、團隊合作、抗壓力、問題解決等重要職能的增進。魏延斌等人（2010）則檢視教學如何培育學生創造力這個重要議題。藉前述課堂教學創新實作研究可發現，強化學生的能力項目與UCAN中的八項職場共通職能相呼應。

當代大學的建立以學術研究與教學為重心（金耀基，1983），身負科學發展與文明進步的使命，目前不可能冀求其全然轉變為同等於技職體系的職人教育，這也不盡符合整體教育體系的分工。然而因應時代需求，傳統大學藉教學創新的應用，培育學生有利進入就業市場的條件，同時兼顧學生的知識成長和工作能力，相信是可以追求的目標。

大學階段的職業能力學習，可能透過在學時自行嘗試的社團或打工經歷（張松年等人，2008），或者以產學合作為主題的學程設計（沈慶龍，2019），以及學系制定的實習規劃（趙惠玉，2016）。更可將職能的概念延伸結合至學系的課程地圖設計（潘瑛如、李隆盛、黃藍瑩，2014）、或者學系專業能力指標訂定（陳淑敏、宋明娟、甄曉蘭，2010）。

綜觀之，不論透過實習、學程、學系、或學生自主歷練，大學內是有工具與資源來培育學生就職能發展的能量，只是過去學校在設定大學應培養學生哪些基本能力之時較忽略職能這一塊（王玫婷、葛惠敏、李隆盛，2017）。本研究目的即試圖探討，大學內推動教學創新課程，所增進的效益不只是課程或專業知識取得，而是透過這些創新的教學設計對學生造成啟發，是否可能發展有利學生未來進入職場的能力，達到從「知識」到「能力」的學習成效目標。

參、研究方法

本研究主要目的在於探討當前大學教育裡著力推行的教學創新概念，在課程的實踐過程中，能有提升學生職能增進的效益，充實未來的職場競爭力。為求此應用型研究之廣度，從議題設定至研究過程取徑於校務研究之實際應用，希望產出的資訊可供未來高教發展教學創新理念時有更充分的基礎。由於校務問題向來複雜，校務研究經常仰賴多元資料來處理問題，以求所獲資訊能夠廣泛運用（彭森明，2018，p. 8）。故本研究在方法上透過蒐集不同類型的資料，試圖綜合各個面向探索教學創新與職能發展的關係。

一、研究場域

本研究於某綜合型大學執行，研究標的為該校教學卓越中心主辦的「三創課程」教學補助計畫中，在108學年第2學期通過申請的課程。該計畫每學期接受校內教師投件申請，主旨為開發創意（教育課程）、創新（特色主題）、創業（經營模式）教學策略，投件的教學方案需提出在課程上的特點以及與過往不同的創新之處，以及教學上可符合TBL（team-based learning）、PBL（problem-based learning）、SBL（solution-based learning）、Flipped classroom等相關創新教學模式，經過他校專家學者審查認可則得以通過補助，108-2學期共有61門課程通過補助申請。

二、資料收集

1. 總體面向：

蒐集108-2學期三創課程教學計畫申請書，利用內容分析法，依教育部「大專校院就業職能平台（UCAN）」（https://ucan.moe.edu.tw）八項共通職能的定義與說明進行編碼。

內容分析法能將書面或是口頭材料區分為具有相同意義內容之類別的方法（Morett et al., 2011），在主觀解釋文本資料時透過編碼與辨識主題（themes）或模式之系統分類過程（Hsieh & Shannon, 2005）。在進行編碼的過程，因依據UCAN八項共通職能，故由一位共同作者作為主責編碼者，並帶領其他編碼員進行編碼。

正式編碼前，研究者先以歷史資料為參照，預先收集106-2學期至108-1學期申請通過之計畫書，比較計劃書內容中，提及UCAN官方定義的八項共通職能的結果，以確認共通職能與標榜教學創新的課程，字句與關鍵字標示範例如下：

> 「…檢視花蓮人文資源與觀光友善程度。實際走訪花蓮機場、花蓮火車站、新城火車站（太魯閣）、花蓮港等四個主要入口，以及旅客服務中心與相關公共交通工具如301公車、303公車、台灣好行觀巴等，檢視目前國際旅客友善程度，以及**提出如何改善問題的發想**。（問題解決，編號Pilot_2A9）」
>
> 「…藉此計畫執行過程，加強學生綜觀學習範圍，使學生了解與連結各個會計資訊領域中的**內部控制與電腦稽核**等實務。（資訊科技應用，Pilot_1A4）」

正式研究階段，蒐集108-2申請補助通過的課程計畫書共61件，對課程進行內容分析。先依據UCAN官方定義的八項共通職能設定重要關鍵詞，接著請編碼人員以關鍵詞為準則，並研判字詞與上下文之基本關聯，進行編碼工作。編碼員分成兩組進行，在完成後互相比對，以確立編碼的穩定性（表1）。

依此，可找出每個職能的養成網絡，對於教學端而言，有時未

表1　分組職能編碼比例

組別	溝通表達	持續學習	人際互動	團隊合作	問題解決	創新	工作責任與紀律	資訊科技應用	總次數
A	14.86%	6.58%	13.05%	18.62%	23.79%	12.32%	2.26%	8.52%	2476
B	14.92%	5.17%	13.54%	17.30%	28.00%	11.04%	1.35%	8.68%	3301

必可清楚整理出教學內容與學生能力的關係，內容分析的審視角度有助察覺出教學設計的內容易於導向的職能種類。

綜合以上，共通職能的培育比重研究與分析程序概略如下：

Step1. 蒐集108-2學期三創課程教學計畫書

Step2. 兩組人員根據關鍵詞庫進行編碼

Step3. 依詞頻多寡瞭解各項共通職能的教學投入

Step4. 依教學投入情形比對課程前後測結果

2. 教師面向：

108-2學期通過三創課程教學補助計畫的教師問卷調查，以複選題讓授課教師從八項共通職能裡選擇課程中預期培養的項目。

3. 學生面向：

於108-2學期期中與期末，派員到班級對學生進行UCAN共通職能施測，利用施測分數前後測檢定來瞭解學生在課程後共通職能的變化。

由於歷年來申請計畫補助的課程非常多元，教學內容涵蓋不同領域，為符合本案以教學創新方法的重點，本次施測對象班級主要先從108-2學期有申請通過的課程中，找出過去幾年有數次通過申請的課程，詢問配合施測之意願，此步驟是希望能重點觀察有心投入創新教學的課程。同時發信詢問在預期施測時間內，能夠配合施測的課程。

研究過程中，共有17門課程在學期中參與施測，預期樣本數為842名，惟學期末部分班級無法配合，能夠接受後測課程為10門，有確實完成前後測並納入本次分析之有效樣本筆數為222。

4. 畢業生面向：

為次級資料分析以及初階資料探勘之應用，串接本校UCAN資料庫106年畢業生在離校一年後的調查結果，運用這屆畢業生在校時填答UCAN共通職能的數據結果，比對他們在畢業一年後對於職場所需能力的意見，此次分析之樣本共905筆。

分析依據為畢業生調查中的問項「您覺得學校，除了教授專業知識（主修科系的專業）外，應加強學生以下哪些能力才能做好工作」，例如經統計後發現溝通表達能力被提出的比率佔32.7%為最高，問題解決能力居次佔14.6%，第三為外語能力佔13.3%。

接著將畢業生調查串接該批畢業生在校時填答的UCAN共通職能結果，試圖瞭解不同職能的高低，是否可能影響畢業後建議的項目有所差異。

畢業生職能觀點的究與分析程序概略如下：

Step1. 從UCAN資料庫串聯畢業一年調查結果

Step2. 瞭解畢業生在調查中建議學校的能力培養

Step3. 串接畢業生問卷調查與UCAN共通職能資，進行資料探索與分析。

肆、研究結果

如表2所示，對108-2三創課程教學補助計畫的申請書，經內容分析發現問題解決、團隊合作、溝通表達、人際互動、創新、的比例皆在10%以上，其中以問題解決和團隊合作最高。教師問卷的調查結果與內容分析結果相近，顯示教師在實行教學創新時，對於掌握自身的教學目標很具體，很清楚要讓學生在課程中學習到哪些能力。

從課程的學期前後測的結果（表3），藉由成對樣本t檢定分析後，顯示問題解決、溝通表達、創新三個共通職能的有明顯進步，持續學習則是接近顯著進步。比對教師欲投入課程的能力培育比例和前後測結果，問題解決、溝通表達、創新可說達到適切的教學效果，教師的教學目標有一定的完成度。

與畢業生調查的結果比對，問題解決和溝通表達這兩項能力是畢業生建議最多的能力，整體而言，問題解決與溝通表達這兩項能力的培養在創新教學的角色可說相對重要，且在本次研究顯現這兩項能力受到授課教師高度重視並且有不錯的學習成效。

進一步比對畢業生調查結果和該群畢業生在校時期的UCAN共通職能施測結果之全國常模PR值（Percentage Rank）（表4），試圖多瞭解建議項目和學生職能的關係。結果顯示創新、資訊科技應用、人際互動、團隊合作、工作紀律責任感及時間管理，都是提出有建議此項的學生PR值分數較高，但未達到統計顯著，而溝通表達則是提出建議此項能力的學生分數較低並達到統計顯著。畢業生調查中有關共通職能建議的題項為複選題，表2的畢業調查職能比例排序計算方式為有勾選此項職能的樣本比例，由於時問卷除了與本研究相關的八項共通職能外尚有其他選項，故總比例相加不會是100%。

表2　共通職能的教學投入與成效

共通職能	內容分析（Rank）	教師問卷（Rank）	畢業調查（Rank）	課程前後測
問題解決	26.5%（1）	17.1%（1）	14.6%（2）	顯著
團隊合作	17.7%（2）	16.7%（2）	6.9%（4）	未顯著
溝通表達	15.0%（3）	14.8%（4）	32.7%（1）	顯著
人際互動	13.2%（4）	11.0%（6）	6.7%（5）	未顯著
創新	11.6%（5）	13.1%（5）	4.4%（8）	顯著
資訊科技應用	8.6%（6）	6.1%（7）	5.6%（6）	未顯著
持續學習	5.7%（7）	15.8%（3）	5.0%（6）	未顯著
工作責任與紀律	1.7%（8）	5.4%（8）	9.8%（3）	未顯著

表3　共通職能前後測

共通職能	M2-M1（SD）n=222	*t*	*p*
問題解決	0.090（.590）	2.292	.023*
團隊合作	-0.012（.517）	-0.356	.722
溝通表達	0.087（.571）	2.270	.024*
人際互動	-0.021（.607）	-0.511	.610
創新	0.108（2.585）	2.585	.010*
資訊科技應用	0.036（.599）	0.908	.365
持續學習	0.069（.588）	1.757	.080
工作責任與紀律	-0.050（.508）	-1.470	.143

*$p<0.05$

表4　建議職能項目與畢業生PR值差異

職能	建議此項 M（SD,N）	未建議 M（SD,N）	*t*	*p*
創新	57.80（30.87,112）	54.61（30.23,792）	1.028	.306
持續學習	56.59（30.80,208）	56.49（30.63,696）	0.042	.967
資訊科技應用	60.66（28.95,153）	57.36（30.438,748）	1.272	.205
人際互動	53.23（31.25,291）	50.26（30.87,613）	1.345	.180
團隊合作	56.14（31.08,241）	54.31（30.49,663）	0.786	.432
工作紀律、責任感及時間管理	56.62（29.70,215）	54.05（30.89,689）	1.099	.272
問題解決	59.90（29.18,411）	59.79（29.67,493）	0.056	.956
溝通表達	55.97（29.50,531）	60.97（29.87,373）	-2.488	.013*

*$p<0.05$

伍、結論

一、教學創新課程於培育職能之益處

將三創課程的教學方案進行內容分析，以及授課教師問卷調查之結果視為教學的投入面，可發現創新教學的課程確實在教學的投入面，與培育共通職能有所契合，尤其以「問題解決」為最高，顯示貫徹教學創新的理念，課程中十分重視學生面對實務工作的能力，不希望學習停留在只會讀書的層次。對比學期前後測的結果，學生在「問題解決」、「溝通表達」、「創新」三個項目在信心水準95%底下皆達到統計顯著，意味這三項職能在教與學兩方面有一定的成效，此外「問題解決」、「溝通表達」兩者亦是畢業生調查中，建議學校應加強培育的能力前二順位，顯示其重要性。

有關工作責任與紀律、資訊科技應用、持續學習的部分，「工作責任與紀律」這項職能，無論內容分析或教師問卷，教學投入的程度較低，課程前後測結果也未呈現顯著進步。教學創新的課程大多著重互動、創意、實作等內涵，這項職能顯然不符合教學創新課程的主軸，受重視程度較低應為合理的結果。而「資訊科技應用」的能力，受到課程屬性的影響較高，通常資訊相關的課程比較容易加強這項能力，本次研究的課程並非以資訊類為主，雖然教學創新中運用數位科技輔助教學是一大特點，但教學運用畢竟不等於學生學習，因此在這項職能教學投入的比例在本次研究也不高，前後測結果也未有顯著差異。

「持續學習」能力則是在內容分析與教師問卷出現較大的差異，顯然教師自己認為課程中是希望加強學生持續學習的能力，但在本研究的編碼過程中並未有同樣的高的比例。這可能是本研究是從職能角度來定義「持續學習」，即學生在工作環境中的學習能力，而教師身為教育者，仍偏向以學業的學習為重，在基本意義上不盡相同。此外，「持續學習」是個較廣泛的概念，也許不容易被撰寫於教學計畫中，造成內容分析的編碼方式和教師本身的意見與想法出現差異，從課程前後測分析結果來看，學生在持續學習的成長是在顯著邊緣，這項能力的增進是否為教學創新課程的強化特點，或是涉及學生個人長期的能力學習，未來仍有探索空間，畢竟不同的課程類型，可能就會對不同的職能有培育作用。

於此可回應研究目的，藉由教學創新課程的推動，可能對於學生未來就業的部分共通職能有增進效益。在綜合型大學的教育型態中，雖然未必以職業訓練為主軸，然而學校或學系除了專注於專業職能的教學外，透過課程的設計與創新培育學生的某些共通職能，應有益於學生未來在職涯上的發展。

二、次級資料探索與職能輔導

校務研究強調校務資料應用於挖掘實際問題以及作為規劃依據，本次研究結合畢業生調查與UCAN共通職能的數據進行分析，發現畢業生建議學校培育的能力的比例最高為「溝通表達」，進一步分析後更發現建議「溝通表達」的學生，在校時期職能施測的統計結果在「溝通表達」明顯較弱。

本次分析所用的畢業生資料為106學年畢業生畢業一年後的調查，畢業一年內是社會新鮮人積極求職或者剛踏入職場的階段，很可能在這個從校園到社會的變化期，面對的人事物和學師生時代的環境大相逕庭，特別感受到溝通表達不足帶來的問題。校方的職涯輔導單位可以考量針對應屆畢生，在溝通表達的問題進行輔導，提升學生對即將面臨的社會生涯的認知，在即將畢業時期增加心理建設與社會溝通技巧。更者，各類教學創新方案的開發，亦能幫助選課的學生增加溝通表達能力，校方亦可推動課程或學程，更多納入教學創新的思維與教法，廣泛地增進學生的相關職能。

資料探勘技術與思維逐漸為當前社會科學研究的利器（羅凱揚、蘇宇暉、鍾皓軒，2021），如大數據、資料庫運用、透過多樣資料結合進行議題推導等等亦屬校務研究範疇的要素（何榮桂，2017）。惟在實務執行上，不同資料的連貫性以及適當的議題結合並不容易，本研究使用UCAN與校務資料庫中的畢業生調查進行結合，找出有關共通職能的資訊進行分析，希望未來在校務研究工作上持續嘗試各類資料科學的應用，擴展更多研究上的可能性。

三、研究限制

本研究過程主要限制為共通職能的課程前後測無法涵蓋所有三創課程，對課程進行前後測本身就需較高的人力與時間成本，更重要者進課堂前後測必須取得該班教師與學生充分的配合意願與現實情況，許多課程可配合前測但到了學期末則無法配合後測。或者到班後部分學生個人覺得已經完成過這個施測，便無意願重複一次。另外在研究執行期間，為配合新冠肺炎的防疫措施，有些班級因授課時間異動而無法配合，以及有些班級採取部分學生於教室上課，部分利用視訊連線，這也造成前後測時班上的成員不同，不少學生僅能完成一次施測，無法納入本次分析之有效樣本。本次前後測結果以管理學院的施測較完整，樣本數比例較高。未來相關的校務研究或者創新教學的分析，若能對各類領域的課程持續探討，對於瞭解此議題必能有更多幫助。

此外，本研究在研究設計上以三創課程為主，並未進一步比較UCAN八項共通職能在一般課程的差異，故未來研究建議可再與一般課程進行比較，對三創教育在高教課程設計實施的實際情況，也能作為檢視大學生在從事不同職業時都需具備能力之程度的檢視，有助於其對職涯發展做出適宜之規劃。

參考文獻

王玫婷、葛惠敏、李隆盛（2017）。普通大學校訂基本素養與學生養成能力之契合度分析。**課程與教學，20**（1），73-104。
台灣就業通（2019）。**2019職場新兵體檢大調查**。取自台灣就業通網站：

https://special.taiwanjobs.gov.tw/Internet/2019/Survey/half_1/index.html
何榮桂（2017）。大數據與校務研究。**臺灣教育，708**，2-9。
沈慶龍（2019）。服務行銷就業學程教學規劃與教學成效評估。**人文社會科學研究：教育類，13**（2），65-97。
林志成（2016）。行動智慧導向的教學創新。**台灣教育**，（698），2-10。
金耀基（1983）。**大學之理念**。台北市：時報文化。
張松年、楊淳皓、蔣忠慈（2008）。大學應屆畢業生自我知覺之核心就業力與其關聯因素分析：以國立宜蘭大學為例。**人文及管理學報**，（5），255-301。
郭廸賢、陳羿熏（2019）。創新動態學在課程創新教學之應用解析：逢甲大學課程融入磨課師學習之案例。**習慣領域期刊，10**（1），19-48。
陳淑敏、宋明娟、甄曉蘭（2010）。大學生專業能力指標之發展——以國立臺灣師範大學為例。**高等教育，5**（2），61-100。
楊文華、莊姍姍、李宗政（2011）。三創教育之終極門檻－建構創新營運模式。**朝陽學報，16**，93-103。
楊玉惠（2013）。大專院校學生核心能力發展之探析，**績效與策略研究，10**（2），1-36。
彭森明（2018）。 校務研究的緣起、理念、發展與運作方針，**臺灣校務研究理論與技術**，台北市：高等教育文化事業有限公司。
趙惠玉（2016）。職場共通職能、實習滿意度與就業意願關係之研究。**島嶼觀光研究，9**（2），91-112。
潘瑛如、李隆盛、黃藍瑩（2014）。科技大學學生共通職能表現及其對課程地圖的意涵。**課程與教學，17**（3），39-60。
鄭夙珍、鄭瀛川（2014）。高等教育職能融入教學行動研究－以心理系課程為例。**課程與教學，17**（1），31-60。
盧以琳、黃鼎倫 高等教育（2018）。「創新教學實驗」計畫與課程教學方案之行動研究：以「創意思考與企劃」為例。**發展與前瞻學報**，（19），35-56。
魏延斌、李柏毅、陳煥卿、林信榕（2010）。教師經由專業發展及教學創新提升學生創造力經驗之探究－敘說取向。**彰化師大教育學報**，（17），51-72。

羅凱揚、蘇宇暉、鍾皓軒（2021）。**最強行銷武器：整合行銷研究與資料科學**。台北市：碁峰資訊有限公司。

羅寶鳳（2016）。學教翻轉：翻轉課堂的課程與教學。**課程與教學，19**（4），1-21。

Cremin, T. (2009)Creative Teachers and Creative Teaching. In A. Wilson(ed.), *Creativity in primary education* (pp. 36-46). Exeter: Learning Matters.

Dikici, A. (2013)The adaptation of creativity fostering primary teachers index scale into Turkish. *Education Sciences: Theory & Practice, 13*(1), 318-323.

Education Week (2018). *Education innovation: Results of a national survey*. Retrieved from Education Week Research Center website: https://epe.brightspotcdn.com/a2/c9/7604df83448faec800063b299cfe/innovation-survey-report-education-week.pdf

Halász, G. (2018). Measuring innovation in education: The outcomes of a national education sector innovation survey. *European Journal of Education, 53(4)*, 557-573. doi: 10.1111/ejed.12299

Hsieh, H. F., & Shannon, S. E. (2005). Three approaches to qualitative content analysis. *Qualitative Health Research, 15*(9), 1277-1288. doi: 10.1177/1049732305276687

Kandemir M. A., Tezci, E. Shelley, M., & Demirli, C.(2019). Measurement of creative teaching in mathematics class. *Creativity Research Journal, 31*(3), 1-12. doi: 10.1080/10400419.2019.1641677

Moretti, F., van Vliet, L., Bensing, J., Deledda, G., Mazzi, M., Rimondini, M., … Fletcher, I. (2011). A standardized approach to qualitative content analysis of focus group discussions from different countries. *Patient Education and Counseling, 82*(3), 420-428. doi: 10.1016/j.pec.2011.01.005

Mulder, M., Gulikers, J., Biemans, H., & Wesselinker, R. (2009). The new competence concept in higher education: error or enrichment?. *Journal of European Industrial Training, 33*(8/9), 755-770. doi: 10.1108/03090590910993616

OECD/Eurosta (2018), *Oslo manual 2018: Guidelines for collecting, reporting and using data on innovation*. Retrieved from OECDiLibrary websit: https://www.oecd.org/sti/inno/oslo-manual-2018-info.pdf

Papaleontiou-Louca, E., Varnava-Marouchou, D., Mihai, S., & Konis, E. (2014). Teaching for creativity in universities. *Journal of Education and Human Development, 3*(4), 131-154. doi: 10.15640/jehd.v3n4a13

Sharma, E., & Sharma, S. (2018). Creativity nurturing behavior scale for teachers. *International Journal of Education Management, 32*(6), 1016-1028. doi: 10.1108/IJEM-10-2017-0294

Soh, K (2000). Indexing creativity fostering teacher behavior: A preliminary validation study. *Journal of Creative Behavior, 34*(2), 118-134. doi: 10.1002/j.2162-6057.2000.tb01205.x

Soh, K. (2015) Creativity fostering teacher behaviour around the world: Annotations of studies using the CFTIndex. *Cogent Education, 2*(1), 1034494. doi: 10.1080/2331186X.2015.1034494.

Tassone, V. C., O'Mahony, C., McKenna, E., Eppink, H. J., & Wals, A. E. J.(2018). (Re-)designing higher education curricula in times of systemic dysfunction: a responsible research and innovation perspective. *Higher Education, 76*(2), 337-352. doi: 10.1007/s10734-017-0211-4

U. S. department of education (2016). *Investing in Innovation Fund (i3)*. Retrieved from U. S. Department of Education website: https://www2.ed.gov/programs/innovation/index.html

Uskov, V., Bakken, J. P., Aluri, L., Rachakonda, R., Rayala, N., & Uskova, M. (2018, March 18-20). *Smart pedagogy: Innovative teaching and learning strategies in engineering education*. In 2018 IEEE World Engineering Education Conference (EDUNINE2018) (pp. 1-6). Santa Cruz de Tenerife, Canary Islands, Spain.

Vincent-Lancrin, S., Jacotin, G., Urgel, J., Kar, S., & González-Sancho, C. (2017). *Measuring innovation in education: A journey to the future*. Paris: OECD Publishing. doi: 10. 20769679.

Wesselink, R., Biemans, H. J., Mulder, M., & van den Elsen, E. R. (2007). Competence-based VET as seen by Dutch researchers. *European Journal of Vocational Training, 40*(1), 38-51.

新南向政策下國際專班學生來臺現況之初探

明新學校財團法人明新科技大學校務研究中心主任
林鴻銘

明新學校財團法人明新科技大學校務研究中心博士後研究員
與企業管理系兼任助理教授
池伯尉

壹、前言

依據教育部的統計，自105學年開始，大學一年級生源之減少趨勢已銳不可擋。據估計111學年，大學1年級學生人數將由105學年以前的26至28萬人，首度跌破20萬人，117學年則將更進一步減至16.2萬人之低點（教育部統計處，2020a）。國內生源不足帶給大學經營上的壓力，爰此，招收境外學生被視為減緩少子化衝擊的主要策略之一。[1]

周宛青（2019）綜整臺灣高教國際化之變化，將其大致分為三個階段。第一階段源於2003年起一系列的擴大招收境外生計劃，[2]加

[1] 本文境外學生意指學生入學時以國際學生、陸生、僑生身份入學之學位生與非學位生。

[2] 相關政策包含：2003年教育部提出「促進高等教育國際競爭力專案」；2004年設立「臺灣獎學金」、行政院將「擴大招收外國學生來臺留學」列入「國家發展重點計

上臺灣獎學金的設立，國際學生的數量快速增加。第二階段則開始於2010年陸生三法的通過，[3]陸生迅速躍升為境外生最大來源，正式修讀學位之陸生亦自2011年的928人，逐年增加至2017年的9,462人，短期研修生人數亦於此階段由11,227人，大幅增加為34,114人（陸委會，2021）。第三階段則係以2016年起加強與新南向國家教育交流及招生為主軸，於此階段中不僅東南亞學生來臺就學人數逐年走高，與技職體系結合的新南向產學合作國際專班（後稱國際專班）亦迅速發展。據統計，在推動新南向人才培育計畫後，2016至2019年間，我國來自東南亞的留學生逐年增加，穩坐國際學生第二大來源；2020年，越南更成為了臺灣境外學生之第一大來源國（教育部統計處，2020b）。

然而，相較於過往對於亞洲國家學生到美國留學之推拉因素（張芳全、余民寧，1999）、陸生來臺留學因素（林彥宏，2010），以及國際學生（包含：印度、馬來西亞、日本與泰國）來臺留學適應問題之探究（蔡文榮、陳雅屏，2015；蔡文榮、董家琳，2015；蔡文榮、石裕惠，2015；蔡文榮、許主愛，2013）。以技職體系國際專班學生為主要研究對象，探討學生們選擇來臺留學的主要因素、在臺之處境，以及生活適應情形的研究卻不多見。

教育部「新南向人才培育推動計畫」自2017年1月1日上路至今已有四年多的時間，在政策施行後，國際專班的學生們在臺之處境、影響他們選擇來臺的因素為何？隨著臺灣高教國際化之階段變化，對技職體系科大招收境外生之情況有何影響？為對上述之問題進行初步之探究，本文嘗試利用個案學校所建置之國際專班資料與相關之境外學生學籍資料進行合併，用以描繪「新南向政策」前後，個案學校境外學生的國籍別消長變化。其次則係利用問卷調查

畫」；2009年，教育部推動「萬馬奔騰」計畫。（教育部，2021）

[3] 臺灣於2010年8月19日立法院三讀通過陸生三法，當中包含：「臺灣地區與大陸地區人民關係條例」第22條、「大學法」第25條、「專科學校法」第26條；教育部於2011年1月6日發布「大陸地區人民來臺就讀專科以上學校辦法」及修正發布「大陸地區學歷採認辦法」。

之方式，訪問400位越南國際專班學生，呈現學生們在臺之處境、影響他們選擇來臺留學的主要因素、課業學習狀況，及生活適應情形，作為日後政策及研究之參考。

本文之主要貢獻有三，首先，本文以越南國際專班之學生為主要訪談對象。據統計，我國國際專班的學生來源高比率集中於越南，106學年度新南向國際專班學生入學人數共計2,494人，其中越南籍即佔1,588人（63.67%）；107學年度亦相仿，在入學的3,158人中，來自越南的學生人數合計佔比高達59.06%（監察院，2019），在目前國際專班學生研究相對較少的情況下，實有瞭解學生們在臺學習適應情形的必要。

其次，依據內政部移民署之統計，截至2020年12月底，除大陸、港澳地區配偶（佔65.43%）外，我國外籍配偶之原屬國籍別以越南為最高（佔19.58%），比率甚至超越了印尼、泰國、菲律賓、柬埔寨、日本、韓國，與其他國家7類之加總（佔14.99%）（移民署，2021）。加上目前國內新住民子女之父（母）來源國家，除大陸地區（約13.7萬人，佔44%）外，亦是以越南籍為最高（約11萬人，佔35.3%）（教育部，2020）。即早了解越南籍學生們來臺留學的處境及適應情況，將有助我國「新南向政策推動計畫」對於東南亞國家新移民及其子女教育政策之擬定。

第三，本文係目前少數兼具學生樣本為單一國籍別與大樣本特性之研究。改善了過往文獻針對單一國籍別學生之研究結果，多為深度訪談與質性方法所做的歸納，在外推性上之限制；或是以多國籍別學生收集之大樣本資料，在相關量化研究時，可能產生不同國別之學生需求互相抵銷，進而導致錯誤或無意義的統計結果的情況（溫子欣，2019）。

貳、文獻探討

一、學生選擇出國求學之影響因素

推拉理論（push-pull theory）為過去探討境外學生來臺求學影響因素時，最主要之理論架構。推拉理論最初之應用為解釋人口之遷移行動，理論認為不論是原居地或移居地，均存在著許多的促使人移入的正向因素（拉力），與促使人移出的負向因素（推力），當移居地的拉力大於原居地，將產生人口遷移，惟當中仍存在干擾因素（例如：距離、移民法規，或遷移搬運費用等）與個人因素（例如：年齡、性別對環境的認知，或訊息的掌握等）交互作用之影響（黃庭玫，2019）。

將上述之理論應用於境外學生流動，詹盛如（2017）指出，對境外學生而言常見的推力因素包含：母國自身教育設施落後、缺乏研究基礎、高等教育受教機會有限、外國學位比較值錢、族群歧視，或是政治不穩定等；至於拉力因素則為：留學國提供豐富的留學獎學金、良善的教育設施、先進的研究環境、就讀大學機會多、財務支持充足、政治穩定，以及學生希望經歷外國生活等。

Roberts、Chou與Ching（2010）以團體訪談和問卷的方式，合計訪問了政治大學來自17個國家的88位國際學生。其中，問卷分析（共45人受訪）結果顯示，臺灣政府提供的獎學金（27%）與高品質的中文課程（19%）為學生們選擇來臺最重要的因素。此外，安全（14%）、臺灣是高科技現代國家（13%）、民主和政治穩定（10%），以及想學習繁體中文（9%）亦為學生們選擇來臺之正向影響因素。在為何選擇就讀政治大學的部份，朋友與同學的推薦（21%）是學生們選擇學校時最重要的原因，其次則分別為學習中文（20%）與大使館或文化辦公室的推薦（18%）。

雖然前者之結論僅以單一學校之國際學生為樣本，不宜作過度的推論，但上述針對不同國籍別國際學生選擇來臺之正向影響因素，進一步在馬藹萱（2014）的大型量化研究中獲得支持。馬藹萱（2014）利用2007至2008年所進行之全臺國際學生問卷調查，以及在北、中、南三區所執行的7場國際學生焦點團體訪談資料，兩部份資料探討國際學生選擇來臺就讀之影響因素。文中問卷以多階段隨機抽樣法進行，共發出987份問卷，回收682份，剔除無效問卷後之有效問卷數為643份。分析結果顯示，學術文化面向因素為國際學生選擇來臺求學時最常考量之因素（僅有8.9%表示從未考慮），其次則為經濟面向因素（28.1%表示從未考慮）與社會面向因素（55.2%表示從未考慮）。比較問卷中上述三個面向涵蓋各項具體因素被勾選的次數，結果顯示，被勾選頻率最高的五項依序為「臺灣的學術資源與品質」、「臺灣的華語文化環境」、「臺灣提供充足的獎學金」、「臺灣學費低廉」，與「臺灣的生活品質」。

另外，馬藹萱（2014）亦利用羅吉斯迴歸（Logistic regression）分析人口學變項之差異對於國際學生來臺考量因素之影響，其中與本文較為相關的重要結論有四：首先，在以日韓為對照組的情況下，亞洲其他國家和其他國家的學生因為臺灣的學術環境而來臺的可能性，將近是日韓學生的4倍，而歐美已開發國家則和日韓無明顯差異；其次，從日韓和歐美已開發國家來臺的國際學生，相對於亞洲其他國家和其他國家的學生，更傾向是基於文化因素而選擇來臺；第三，不論是亞洲其他國家或其他國家的學生，相較於來日韓和歐美已開發國家的國際學生，他們因為臺灣就學成本低廉而選擇來臺就讀的可能性較低；最後，相對於日韓和歐美的學生，亞洲其他國家和其他國家的學生，明顯更為積極地回應臺灣提供獎學金所形成的拉力效應。

與Roberts、Chou與Ching（2010）及馬藹萱（2014）之樣本主體為國際學生不同。Nghia（2015）則是在以越南學生為主體的情況下，探討學生們出國留學的影響因素。文中研究設計共分為兩個階段，第一階段作者先以訪談的方式收集55位準留學生選擇留學國家和學校的影響因子，做為問卷設計之參考資料，再以第一階段之基礎，收集400份問卷進行量化資料分析。研究中對於越南學生選擇留學目的地與學校之主要發現包含：

1. 越南學生對於留學目的地的選擇，開始逐漸從美國和澳洲等西方國家，移往日本和新加坡等亞洲國家。
2. 尋求移民機會與教育品質低落為學生們由越南轉至其他國家留學主要的推力因素，增加國際性之就業機會、增進語言能力和獲取國際經驗等則為其他國家對越南國際學生之拉力因素。
3. 留學目的地的文化有趣、生活成本，以及對於國際學生的兼職政策，為學生們選擇留學目的地時最常考量的因素。
4. 相較於大學的聲譽／排名、是否能讀到想要的科系，與學校是否具備合格的師資質量，學生們在選擇學校時更在意畢業後的就業率。
5. 對於周遭旁人的意見，學生們在選擇學校時最在意的是過往留學生的經驗，其次則為當地雇主的偏好，廣告宣傳或家人／朋友的意見則為排序較後面之影響因素。

陳淑慧等人（2018）、張芳全（2017）與Thai（2013）進一步將研究對象限縮為東南亞或越南籍的學生，探討學生們來臺留學的相關因素，而潘俊宏與張仁家（2019）則是以文獻探討搭配政府機構數據資料的方式，呈現國際學生選擇來臺留學的主要因素。

陳淑慧等人（2018）針對新南向國家之菲律賓、馬來西亞、越南，實際到當地與大學生進行問卷調查與深度訪談並加以分析。由作者們的分析結果顯示：

1. 對菲律賓、馬來西亞、越南三個國家來說華語教學是具備吸引力的，尤其臺灣本身提供的華語環境與課程是受訪學生想來台的主要原因之一；進一步分析得知推出華語文教學，對越南學生的拉力比菲律賓要大，且越南學生較偏好全中文之學習環境。

2. 在經濟層面，生活花費是受訪學生重要考量因素，若能有獎學金將可提升來臺就讀意願。此外，越南學生特別重視就業機會，從作者們進行深度訪談的29份問卷中，有23份提及了未來就業機會的重要性。
3. 受訪的學生認為自己國家有崇尚出國學習之風氣，其中，最重要的是若臺灣能夠在校園內外提供友善國際生學習環境，生活條件的奧援，將可有效的提升來臺意願。而相關奧援包括：簡化相關的就業、居留程序，或者給予主動積極的協助，將使國際生強化就讀學習的態度。

張芳全（2017）訪談13位來自東南亞的學生，藉以瞭解東南亞國家的學生們來臺留學的相關因素。作者指出影響學生們來臺留學主要之拉力因素包含：兩國的距離近、文化相近、臺灣的生活水準高、臺灣入學條件較寬、兩國的貿易增加、臺灣提供獎學金，與畢業後想留在臺灣等；學生們離開原居住國之主要因素則包含：想出國體驗、學習華語文、臺灣高等教育品質比東南亞國家好、臺灣大學制度較優異（如：東南亞國家大學入學條件嚴格及行政手續不完善），以及部份國家（如：馬來西亞）有排華現象等。Thai（2013）訪談17位在臺灣攻讀碩士和博士學位的越南學生，在越南的推力與臺灣的拉力因素部份與前述文獻相似，亦不脫離想出國體驗、臺灣提供豐富的獎學金，海外教育的品質較佳等範疇。但較為特殊的是，作者亦於研究中指出了對於來臺留學的越南籍學生們來說，至其他國家留學的推力因素，其中包含：英語系國家需要較高的英文水準、在競爭激烈的情況下難以申請經濟協助與學生簽證。最後，潘俊宏與張仁家（2019）指出，近年增強國際學生來臺留學動機之主要因素大致可歸納為：臺灣的獎學金政策；地理位置鄰近東南亞國家；近年來政府推動「新南向政策」。

綜合上述文獻顯示，對境外學生而言，常見的推力因素大致包含：母國自身教育品質較為低落、學生想增加國際經驗，或是族群歧視等；至於拉力因素則為：留學國提供豐富的留學獎學金、國外環境生活水準較佳等。惟不同國家或地區之國際學生，他們在選擇留學國時之影響因素，可能仍存在些許之差異，例如：日韓和歐美國家的學生，可能更傾向考慮留學國之文化因素；經濟面向因素多為東南亞國家學生們考量。臺灣對境外學生留學之獎學金政策已施行多年，加上近年政府積極推動「新南向政策」，豐富的留學獎學金、華語文化的學習環境，以及地理位置鄰近東南亞國家，成為我國推動高教國際化吸引境外學生前來就讀，重要的拉力因素。

二、境外學生赴臺之適應情形

臺灣因為豐富的留學獎學金、生活的便利性，以及獨特的華語文化環境等原因，廣受國際學生歡迎。據統計境外學生人數亦從2007年之30,509人，逐年提升至2019年的128,157人（教育部統計處，2019）。然而，隨著境外學生人數的逐年上升，學生們在臺灣的處境、適應，與就學困難等問題也隨之浮現。

在境外學生來臺灣就學所需面對的諸多困難中，導因於中文能力對學習適應所造成的影響，與學生們來臺後的人際關係及生活適應，為目前既有的相關文獻中最常發現的問題。

首先在中文能力的部份，Pham、Wu 與 Blohm （2017）針對暨南大學50位國際學生之學習滿意度進行分析，他們的研究結果顯示，雖然學生們具有性別、母國別、停留在台灣期間的長短、專攻學門、英文程度，與教育程度等人口學變項的差異，但上述因子對學生們的專業科目學習滿意度與整體滿意度均沒有顯著的影響，而學生們的中文程度愈高，其滿意度亦越高。作者們指出，雖然校園國際化與全英語授課之推動在臺灣已行之有年，但多數的課程與校園活動仍是以中文為主，因此國際學生們的中文程度對他們的學習經驗與學習滿意度均具有顯著的影響。這樣的結果與馬藹萱（2014）指出，當國際學生的中文能力愈高，就愈有機會瞭解臺灣的生活情況，愈有能力使用臺灣社會的各樣資源，在臺灣生活也會相對更加便利的觀點相互呼應。

值得注意的是，雖然Pham、Wu與Blohm（2017）僅以單一學校之國際生為研究樣本，但他們的結論亦在國內多所學校對國際學生之學習經驗分析中得到支持。例如：蔡文榮與巫麗芳（2013）、蔡文榮與徐主愛（2013）、蔡文榮與石裕惠（2015），以及蔡文榮與陳雅屏（2015）分別對中興大學來自越南、泰國、日本與印度的國際學生所進行的訪談研究，研究結果相當一致的顯示，語言上的障礙會對學生們的學習適應形成負面的影響。另外，吳娟與彭貞淑（2017）針對輔仁大學116位國際學生的學習經驗的調查研究發現，約半數的國際學生認為中文程度影響了他們在學期報告、理解學術演講內容，以及進行口頭報告的學習經驗。

在境外學生們來臺後的人際關係及生活適應部份，目前既有文獻之研究結果顯示，與臺灣學生的社交互動因學生們的來源國而存在差異。周宛青（2019）指出，雖然目前境外學生對臺灣社會的感受多為正面，但既存的刻板印象仍對學生們造成困擾。作者指出，不少參與其過往研究計畫之陸生及東南亞生，都曾遇到負面刻板印象或被歧視的事件，例如：店家意識到不同口音後，表示「產品只賣臺灣人」的事件。另外，蔡文榮與徐主愛（2013）針對泰國學生所做的研究指出，大部份的泰國學生來臺後常常會感到寂寞與孤單，並覺得臺灣的學生比較冷漠。研究結果也發現沒有任何泰國學生有臺灣的學生為親密朋友。大部份泰國學生的親密朋友都是來自泰國的同學，在生活方面不管是要一起去玩，一起去吃飯，他們都是常常跟著泰國同學一起，有問題時也是與泰國的學長和學姐商量。然而，上述不易結交朋友或被社交圈接納的現象，卻未出現於日本籍留學生的研究中。蔡文榮與石裕惠（2015）針對日本籍國際學生的研究結果顯示，日本籍國際學生在臺灣的大學求學過程中，結交朋友的問題並不明顯，反而都結交了許多臺灣的朋友。

綜合上述文獻之結果，顯示國際學生們的中文能力將對其來臺後的學習適應造成影響，為目前研究普遍一致性之結論。但在學生們來臺後的人際關係及生活適應的部份，既存文獻顯示，陸生或東南亞國家學生與臺灣學生有所距離，較難發展社交關係，甚至可感受到排斥或是異樣的眼光。但上述的情況並未出現於日本籍留學生的研究中，表示來自不同國家或地區之學生與本國學生在社交互動關係上可能有所差異。

參、資料來源與問卷設計

一、資料來源

本文的資料共分為兩部份，第一部分為個案學校校內資料倉儲中所建置之國際專班資料與境外學生學籍資料。當中包含了102至109學年度境外學生之原屬國籍別與入學方式，用以描繪「新南向政策」前後境外學生的國籍別消長變化。第二部份資料為問卷資料，旨在探討個案學校之越南國際專班，學生們的赴臺就讀動機、課業學習與生活適應狀況。

二、問卷設計與受訪對象

本文之問卷共分為基本資料、出國念書之動機與相關資訊、課業學習適應狀況，與生活適應狀況四個部份。其中，為求問卷內容符合內容效度（content validity），本研究之問卷設計過程邀請了個案學校國際處承辦人員以其專業知識協助中文問卷之修改，並透過校內已考取A級中文檢定證照之越南籍同學進行翻譯。最後，為增加翻譯後之越南版本問卷在文字與修辭之嚴謹性，本研究尚委請個案學校之越南籍同學進行試訪，完成問卷之最終版本。

目前個案學校招收國際專班之班別分為春季班及秋季班，二者之主要差異為入學時間不同。暑假後入學者為秋季班，寒假後入學者則為春季班，國際專班學生入學後的第一年均在學校修課，從第二年開始實習，實習開始後會選定固定時間回學校上課。

鑒於學生參與實習後聯絡不易，本研究以2019年6月時，個案學校工學院尚未參與實習之越南國際專班學生為訪談對象，其中包含：106學年度之秋季班（106下學期入學）1班、107學年度秋季班（107上學期入學）4班，與107學年春季班（107下學期入學）3班，共計586人。本研究於2019年6月，對上述受訪範圍之對象進行調查，於課堂中徵求任課老師同意後進行問卷發放，排除不願受訪之班級，總計發出400份問卷，回收400份，其中有效問卷共338份，有效回收率為84.5%。各面向信度分析之Cronbach's Alpha值均達0.7以上（Hee, 2014）。

我們將受訪學生的基本資料呈現於表1。由表1可見，本文之受訪學生以男性居多，佔62.4%，這可能與個案學校之國際專班科系以理工相關科系居多有關。學生們的年齡分佈主要為18-22歲（含），佔85.2%，與一般就讀大學之年紀相符。在就讀科系的分佈上，以化材系與機械系為最多，其次則分別為電子系與電機系。整體而言，國際專班的學生們於課餘時間均有打工之經驗，其中以平均一週打工時間12個小時以上為最多，佔31.1%。在每月生活費的部份，以5,000元以下及5,000-10,000元為最多，約各佔40%。

表1　受訪學生基本資料（N=338）

	人數	百分比
性別		
男	211	62.4
女	127	37.6
年齡		
18歲~22歲（含）	288	85.2
22歲~26歲（含）	45	13.3
26歲以上	5	1.5
就讀科系		
化材系	95	28.1
機械系	94	27.8
電子系	59	17.5
電機系	50	14.8
光電系	40	11.8
平均一週打工時數		
8小時（含）以下	95	28.1
8-10（含）小時	66	19.5
10-12（含）小時	72	21.3
12小時以上	105	31.1
每月生活費		
5,000元以下	154	45.6
5,000-10,000元	141	41.7
10,000-15,000元	38	11.2
1,5000元以上	5	1.5

肆、結論

一、境外學生入學趨勢分析

圖1所呈現的是102至109學年度個案學校境外學生之入學人數

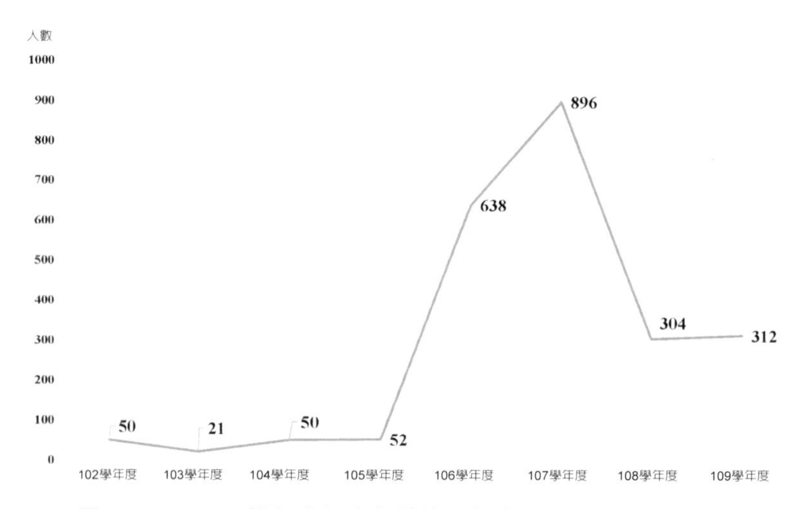

圖1　102至109學年度個案學校境外學生之入學人數趨勢變化

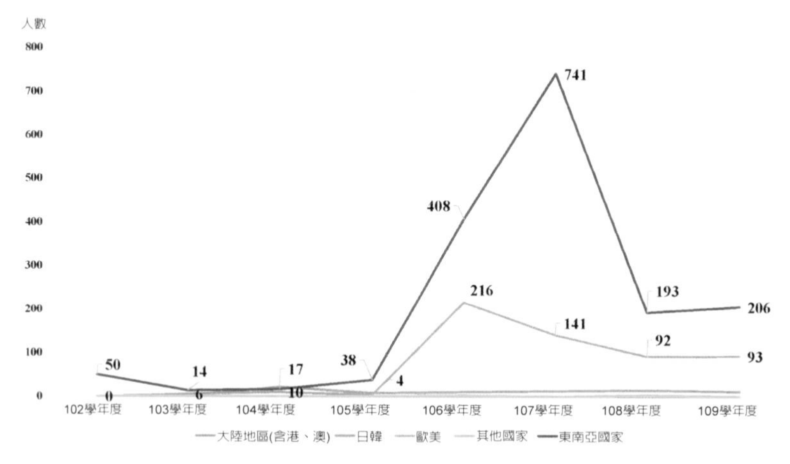

圖2　個案學校境外生入學人數分佈趨勢

趨勢變化。由圖可見，個案學校境外學生之入學人數大致可分為三個區段：第一個區段為102至105學年度，在此區段，學生人數大致為平穩狀態，歷年入學人數約在100人以下；第二個區段則為，106

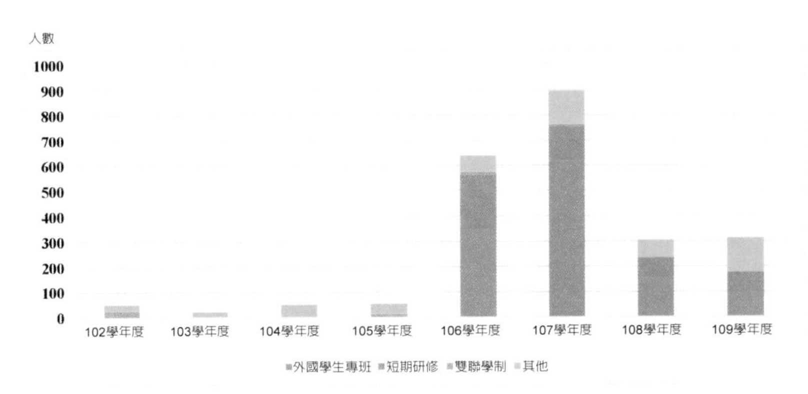

圖3　個案學校境外生入學人數分佈趨勢_以來源國區分

至107學年度，此階段為境外學生入學人數大幅成長之階段，由原先105學年度之52人成長至106學年度的638人，107學年度更進一步成長至896人；最後則是108至109學年度，此階段境外學生入學人數較107學年度下降約67%，108學年度之境外學生入學人數為304人。

本文將102學年度至109學年度，個案學校境外學生之入學人數以來源國進行區分，呈現於圖2。由圖2可見，102至105學年度間，境外學生之來源國分佈差異並不明顯。然而到了106學年度，大陸地區（含港澳）與東南亞國家之學生入學人數大幅上升，107學年度東南亞國家學生入學人數則進一步上升至新高，惟大陸地區（含港澳）之學生入學人數下降。108至109學年度境外學生入學人數下降，但來源國維持以東南亞國家之學生為主。圖3所呈現的則是102至109學年度，個案學校之境外學生入學方式。由圖3可見，在個案學校境外學生入學人數大幅成長之階段，主要之生源入學方式以外國學生專班為主，其次則是短期研修。

我們將個案學校境外學生入學人數之變化趨勢與我國教育政策，及大環境因素進行對照。可以發現在我國教育政策推動高教國際化之初期，雖然政府鼓勵擴大招收國際學生，但個案學校在此階段較不具明顯之競爭優勢，歷年入學之境外學生雖有，但大致均維持於100人以下。個案學校境外學生入學人數大幅成長之階段，則對應了我國開放陸生來臺研修及修讀學位後，研修生人數與學位生人數最高的階段，[4]以及新南向國家教育政策推動後。顯示，在教育政策上陸生三法的通過，與新南向國家教育政策的推動，確實有助於個案學校透過招收境外學生增加生源。另外，108至109學年度個案學校境外生入學人數大幅下降之階段，則對應了全球Covid-19疫情爆發之時間點。

整體而言，雖然招收境外學生普遍被視為減緩少子化衝擊的策略，但對於境外學生的招收，除了學校端必須策略性的選擇國際化定位、考量校內的行政與教學配套措施，及招生量能外，整體之招收狀況仍與教育政策走向及整體環境之影響因子（如：疫情）有著密不可分的關係。

二、出國念書動機、赴臺與選擇個案學校原因

鑒於目前兼具學生樣本為單一國籍別與大樣本特性之國際學生研究並不多見，本文以個案學校工學院越南國際專班之學生為問卷訪談對象，探討學生們的赴臺就讀動機、課業學習與生活適應狀況。其中，因為詢問學生們來臺主要原因的題組設計目的，在於瞭解在臺學生們當初來臺的動機。考量他們在決策形成與學習選擇上可能存在多元考量的情況，因此本研究於此部份之題目設計均為複選題。

表2結果顯示，對於越南籍的學生們來說，提升未來就業競爭力（78.4%）為學生們出國念書最主要的動機，其次則分別為學習他國語言（59.2%）以及增加學習機會（47%），排序最後的則是想

[4] 依據我國陸委會之統計，2014至2017年為研修生入境數最高的幾年，2018年起開始逐年下滑（陸委會，2021）。

多了解其他國家文化（36.7%）。這樣的結果，與Nghia（2015）指出，對越南學生們而言留學國主要之拉力因素為增加國際性之就業機會、增進語言能力和獲取國際經驗，以及陳淑慧等人（2018）探討東南亞學生來臺因素時，發現越南學生們在經濟層面特別注重未來就業機會的結果相符。

在為何選擇到臺灣留學的問項中，本文之統計結果顯示，喜歡臺灣文化（49.1%）、離越南較近（41.7%）、生活成本低（41.7%），與臺灣政府的優惠策略（36.4%），是越南學生們選擇到臺灣原因排序的前三順位。呼應了潘俊宏與張仁家（2019）指出，臺灣的獎學金政策、地理位置鄰近東南亞國家，以及政府推動之「新南向政策」，為近年增強國際學生來臺留學動機之三大重要因素的看法，亦與張芳全（2017）針對東南亞學生所進行的質性訪談結果相似。

在學生們選擇就讀個案學校原因的部份，近6成的學生指出個案學校具有較多研究學習（工讀）的機會（58.9%）為他們選擇就讀的主因，其次則分別為個案學校的課程及畢業條件較容易達成（52.9%），以及畢業後較容易找到工作（47.6%）。這樣的結果呼應了Nghia（2015）發現，國際學生的兼職政策，為越南學生們選擇留學目的地時最常考量的因素；另外，相對於大學的聲譽／排名、是否能讀到想要的科系，與學校是否具備合格的師資質量，學生們在選擇學校時更在意畢業後的就業率。惟需特別留意的是，本文之研究對象主要係科技大學新南向國際專班的學生，而專班之主要目的為與企業合作辦理客製化產學合作，以培育當地產業所需人才為臺商所用，或留任於產學合作廠商就業，為我國企業挹注新助力。此部份學制上的差異，可能導致學生在填答選擇動機時，更為偏向對於工作機會的重視，與一般學制之學生略有不同。

我們進一步利用1.「選擇個案學校的資訊來源」、2.「是否推薦親友到個案學校就讀」、3.「推薦原因」、4.「除了台灣，到越南招生有哪些國家」，與5.「除了台灣，曾想到哪些國家讀書」等5個問項，希望瞭解個案學校在新南向國際專班的招生優勢與未來在招生時可能遇到的潛在競爭國家。研究結果顯示，半數以上的學生們獲得個案學校相關資訊的訊息管道為親友介紹（51.5%），其次為仲介介紹（35.2%），透過網路獲取資訊與參加臺灣高等教育展覽會則分別為25.2%與9.5%。與Roberts、Chou與Ching（2010）發現，朋友與同學的推薦是學生們選擇學校時最重要原因的結果相同。

本文之研究結果顯示，約有83.4%的學生願意持續推薦親友至個案學校就讀。有趣的是，進一步觀察促使學生們願意推薦親友就讀的原因，絕大多數與友善的校園環境有關，其中包含：學校與師長非常照顧國際學生（66.3%）、學校設備與住宿環境佳（50%）、學校的地理位置較佳（50%）、本地生對國際學生很友善（49.4%），以及華語教學制度完善（44.1%）。畢業後較容易找到工作以及課程與畢業條件較容易達成，這類當初學生們選擇就讀個案學校的原因，反而成為了排序較為後面的推薦原因。驗證了陳淑慧等人（2018）指出，若臺灣能夠在校園內外提供友善的國際生學習環境與生活條件奧援，將可有效提升東南亞學生來臺意願。

透過「除了臺灣，到越南招生有哪些國家」，與「除了臺灣，曾想到哪些國家讀書」2個問項的填答，我們可以發現日本可能為臺灣學校在越南招生時，最大的潛在競爭對手。在學生的回覆中，不僅有高達81.7%的學生表示日本曾至當地招生，亦有64.5%的學生表示曾想到日本留學，反觀曾想至中國大陸留學的學生，只佔了13.9%。這樣的結果亦呼應了Nghia（2015）發現，越南學生對於留學目的地的選擇，開始逐漸從美國和澳洲等西方國家，移往日本和新加坡等亞洲國家的現象。

最後，本文之分析結果顯示，學生們對未來的規劃主要仍是以留在臺灣為首要之考量，計有約60%以上的學生希望能繼續留在臺灣就業或升學，僅有約27%的學生對未來之規畫為回到越南就業或升學。

表2　學生出國念書動機、赴臺與選擇個案學校原因（N=338）

問項	人數	百分比
出國念書動機（複選題）		
提高未來就業競爭	265	78.4
可以學習他國語言	200	59.2
可增加學習機會	159	47
想打工賺錢	127	37.6
想多了解其他國家文化	124	36.7
選擇來臺灣留學原因（複選題）		
喜歡台灣文化	166	49.1
離越南較近	141	41.7
生活成本低	141	41.7
台灣政府的優惠策略	123	36.4
親友也在台灣唸書	116	34.3
台灣學歷較有價值	105	31.1
申請簽證較容易通過	87	25.7
選擇就讀明新科技大學的原因（複選題）		
明新科技大學具有較多研究學習（工讀）的機會	199	58.9
明新科技大學的課程及畢業條件較容易達成	179	52.9
畢業後較容易找到工作	161	47.6
考量明新科技大學的地理位置	99	29.3
參考明新科技大學的世界排名	80	23.7
考量明新科技大學的獎學金及學費制度	69	20.4
獲知明新科技大學的訊息管道（複選題）		
親友介紹	174	51.5
仲介介紹	119	35.2
透過網路獲取資訊	85	25.2
參加台灣高等教育展覽會	32	9.5
其他	34	10.1
是否會推薦親友就讀明新科技大學		
是	282	83.4
否	56	16.6

問項	人數	百分比
願意持續推薦親友就讀明新科技大學的原因（複選題）		
學校與師長非常照顧外籍生	224	66.3
學校設備與住宿環境佳	169	50
本地生對外籍生很友善	167	49.4
學校的地理位置較佳	169	50
華語教學制度完善	149	44.1
畢業後較容易找到工作	121	35.8
課程與畢業條件較容易達成	80	23.7
明新科大的學歷較具優勢	69	20.4
獎學金制度較完善	67	19.8
其他	12	3.6
除了臺灣，到越南招生有哪些國家（複選題）		
日本	276	81.7
韓國	226	66.9
中國大陸	75	22.2
除了臺灣，曾想到哪些國家讀書（複選題）		
日本	218	64.5
韓國	152	45
中國大陸	47	13.9
未來生涯規劃		
留在台灣就業	152	44.9
留在台灣念書	70	20.7
回越南就業	61	18.1
回越南念書	31	9.2
其他	24	7.1

三、學生們的課業與生活適應

在國際學生們的課業適應部份。表3之結果顯示，有73.7%的學生認為「臺灣的教學方式與越南差異很大」（同意與非常同意），並有79.9%的學生指出自己在課業學習中曾經主動尋求過師長的幫助。但僅有約60%的學生在「我能夠如期完成授課老師交代的作業」的問項中表示同意，而同意「我認為達到授課老師的期望與標準是簡單的」更僅有42%。由此可知，教學方式的轉變可能是學生們來臺後在課業適應上主要面對的困難，此部份係目前既有文獻針對國際學生學習適應分析較少提到的部份。此外，研究結果也顯示，約有65%以上的學生認為在個案大學上課對其中文進步很大，呼應了薛家明（2015）指出，在考慮到本地生的英文能力尚待加強，且所收的境外學生英文並不是那麼好的情況下，可透過語言中心採取華語先修輔導、華語密集班等策略，提升境外學生的中文能力，協助其跟上課程進度的教學策略。

本文以1.「我來臺灣已經結交到本地朋友」、2.「有困難時，除了老師，我找不到願意協助我的本地人」、3.「我覺得本地學生對我們是友善的」、4.「我能勇敢表明自己是國際學生，不在意他人眼光」，與5.「我很習慣在學校的生活」5個問項分析學生們來臺後於校園中之生活與人際適應情形，而此部份之結果為本文與過往文獻之研究結果差異最大的地方。

表3　學生課業適應情形（N=338）

問題	人數	百分比
臺灣的教學方式與越南差異很大。		
非常同意	70	20.7
同意	179	53
普通	82	24.3
不同意	6	1.8
非常不同意	1	0.3
我能夠如期完成授課老師交代的作業。		
非常同意	52	15.4
同意	152	45
普通	116	34.3
不同意	18	5.3
非常不同意	0	0
我認為達到授課老師的期望與標準是簡單的。		
非常同意	23	6.8
同意	119	35.2
普通	172	50.9
不同意	23	6.8
非常不同意	1	0.3
我在課業學習中曾經主動尋求過師長的幫助。		
非常同意	94	27.8
同意	176	52.1
普通	65	19.2
不同意	3	0.9
非常不同意	0	0
我認為在明新科技大學上課對我中文進步很大。		
非常同意	62	18.3
同意	159	47
普通	109	32.3
不同意	7	2.1
非常不同意	1	0.3

透過本文表4之結果可以發現，僅有18.7%的學生不同意「我來臺灣已經結交到本地朋友」之論述，其中，非常不同意之佔比更是僅有1.5%。另外，在「我覺得本地學生對我們是友善的」部份，不同意與非常不同意之佔比分別僅佔1.2%及0.9%；而在「有困難時，除了老師，我找不到願意協助我的本地人」此題，回答同意與非常同意之佔比僅分別為3.9%及3.0%。上述之結果顯示，學生們進入個案學校就讀後，大多均可感到人際環境友善，並結交到本地學生朋友，有困難時亦有除老師以外之協助管道。這樣的結果與周宛青（2019）、蔡文榮與陳雅屏（2015）、以及蔡文榮與徐主愛（2013）的研究結果形成鮮明對比。顯示既存文獻指出，陸生或東南亞國家學生與臺灣學生有所距離，較難發展社交關係，甚至可感受到排斥或是異樣的眼光的結果。然而透過本文的發現，顯示境外生來臺之人際適應情況，除了國籍別間的差異外，亦可透過學校對於校園環境之建構，提升境外學生們的適應情形。

此外，由本研究之調查結果可見，目前就讀個案學校的越南學生，他們在學校當中並不會在意別人的眼光，反而是勇敢做自己，有80%以上的學生表示能勇敢表明自己是國際學生，並有74.3%的學生認為自己很習慣在學校的生活。

最後，本文利用「我能習慣臺灣的天氣變化」、「我能習慣臺灣的飲食」、「我能習慣臺灣的交通狀況」、「我能習慣臺灣的文化習俗」，與「我能接受臺灣人的工作態度」等問項觀察國際學生們在臺灣之生活適應情況。本文之分析結果顯示，國際學生們對臺灣的天氣變化、飲食、交通狀況、文化習俗，與臺灣人的工作態度，感到無法適應（不同意或非常不同意）的比率大致均在10%以下，其中以飲食不適應之比率為最高（約為10.07%）。可能的解釋是，是越南和臺灣除了有一個小時的時差外，在日常生活方面，其實具有相當多的相似之處，例如：越南的代步工具大部份亦多是以機車為主、在文化習俗上，越南人一樣會過春節、中秋節等，因此學生們在日常生活中的食衣住行並無明顯之不適應。

表4　學生人際與生活適應情形（N=338）

問題	人數	百分比
我來台灣已經結交到本地朋友。		
非常同意	38	11.2
同意	108	32
普通	129	38.2
不同意	58	17.2
非常不同意	5	1.5
有困難時，除了老師，我找不到願意協助我的本地人。		
非常同意	10	3
同意	13	3.9
普通	61	18.1
不同意	188	55.6
非常不同意	66	19.5
我覺得本地學生對我們是友善的。		
非常同意	54	16
同意	158	46.8
普通	119	35.2
不同意	4	1.2
非常不同意	3	0.9
我能勇敢表明自己是外籍生，不在意他人眼光。		
非常同意	95	28.1
同意	188	55.6
普通	51	15.1
不同意	2	0.6
非常不同意	2	0.6

問題	人數	百分比
我很習慣在學校的生活。		
非常同意	57	16.9
同意	194	57.4
普通	82	24.3
不同意	3	0.9
非常不同意	2	0.6
我能習慣台灣的天氣變化。		
非常同意	46	13.6
同意	190	56.2
普通	88	26
不同意	11	3.3
非常不同意	3	0.9
我能習慣台灣的飲食。		
非常同意	36	10.7
同意	153	45.3
普通	113	33.4
不同意	27	8
非常不同意	9	2.7
我能習慣台灣的交通狀況。		
非常同意	33	9.8
同意	199	58.9
普通	95	28.1
不同意	8	2.4
非常不同意	3	0.9
我能習慣台灣的文化習俗。		
非常同意	33	9.8
同意	201	59.5
普通	95	28.1
不同意	8	2.4
非常不同意	1	0.3

問題	人數	百分比
我能接受台灣人的工作態度。		
非常同意	42	12.4
同意	210	62.1
普通	76	22.5
不同意	9	2.7
非常不同意	1	0.3

伍、結論與建議

近年來隨著少子化下本國生源持續減少，招收境外學生常被視為有效減緩少子化衝擊的策略之一。然而，透過本研究之分析可見，雖然境外學生某種程度上能夠彌補本國生源的部份缺口，但整體而言仍與國內的教育政策有著密不可分的關係。以本文所分析之個案學校為例，隨著開放陸生來臺研修以及新南向國家教育政策的推動，個案學校之國際生入學人數由原先105學年度之52人，大幅成長至107學年度的896人，然而在Covid-19疫情爆發之後，國際學生入學人數隨即下降約67%。據此，在少子化浪潮襲擊下，透過招收境外學生之做法來舒緩此一壓力無可厚非，但是否需倚重這樣方式做為少子化浪潮下之解藥，仍需在考量學校國際化定位及環境變化後進行審慎評估。

鑒於目前以技職端國際專班學生為主要研究對象，探討學生們選擇來臺留學的主要因素、在臺之處境，以及生活適應情形的研究並不多見。本研究嘗試在避免不同國別之學生需求互相抵銷的情況下，探討越南國際專班的學生們，選擇來臺留學的主要因素、在臺之處境，以及生活適應情形。

本文之研究結果顯示，對於越南學生們來說，他們出國念書最主要的動機為提升未來的就業競爭力，而喜歡臺灣文化、地理位置鄰近其母國、生活成本較低，與臺灣政府的優惠策略，為吸引學生們赴臺留學最重要的拉力因素。此外，研究結果也顯示，學生們選擇就讀個案學校原因的部份，有近6成的學生指出係因具有較多研究學習（工讀）機會，但促使學生們願意推薦親友就讀的原因，絕大多數與友善的校園環境有關。據此，學校在招生策略的擬定上，深耕當地並持守原本立意良善之政策目標以創造更友善、親切的留學環境，才是長遠經營之道。

本文與過往文獻研究結果差異最大的地方在於，境外學生們進入個案學校就讀後，大多均可感到人際環境友善，並結交到本地學生朋友，有困難時亦有除老師以外之協助管道。與既存文獻指出，陸生或東南亞國家學生與臺灣學生有所距離，較難發展社交關係，甚至可感受到排斥或是異樣的眼光的結果不同。顯示除了國籍別間之差異外，學生們的人際適應情形亦可能因學生所處之校園環境不同而有所差異。另外，由於越南和臺灣除了有一個小時的時差外，在日常生活方面，其實具有相當多的相似之處，因此學生們對臺灣的天氣變化、飲食、交通狀況、文化習俗，與臺灣人的工作態度，均無感到明顯的無法適應。

最後，針對本文之結論仍有幾點須讀者特別注意。首先，由於本研究僅以單一科大之學生為研究樣本，因此在整體境外生的招收人數與入學方式上，可能有其外推性之限制。其次，本研究主要係以國際專班之學生為訪談對象，由於國際專班之設立有其目標特殊性，因此學生在填答選擇來臺因素時，就業動機可能較一般學制之學生更為強烈。

參考文獻

教育部統計處（2020a），**各教育階段學生數預測報告（109～124學年度）**。https://depart.moe.edu.tw/ed4500/News_Content.aspx?n=48EBDB3B9D51F2B8&sms=F78B10654B1FDBB5&s=8E751C15DB8BE44C

教育部統計處（2020b），**大專校院境外學生狀況**。http://stats.moe.gov.tw/statedu/chart.aspx?pvalue=3

教育部（2021），**擴大招收境外學生**。https://history.moe.gov.tw/policy.asp?id=18

教育部（2020），**108學年各級學校新住民子女就學概況提要分析**。https://stats.moe.gov.tw/files/analysis/108_son_of_foreign_ana.pdf

陸委會（2021），**陸生來臺研修及修讀學位統計**。https://www.mac.gov.tw/cp.aspx?n=A3C17A7A26BAB048

監察院（2019），**108教正0012號糾正案文**。https://www.cy.gov.tw/CyBsBox.aspx?CSN=2&n=134&_Query=1285a28e-ceb4-4ef3-9b14-f2fc6c742950

內政部移民署（2021），**外籍配偶與大陸（含港澳）配偶人數**。https://www.gender.ey.gov.tw/gecdb/Stat_Statistics_DetailData.aspx?sn=lJvq%2BGDSYHCFfHU73DDedA%3D%3D&d=m9ww9odNZAz2Rc5Ooj%2FwIQ%3D%3D

吳娟、彭貞淑（2017）。Cross border learning: A case study of international students' learning experiences in Fu Jen Catholic University。**全人教育學報，15**，53-83。

林彥宏（2010）。一廂情願抑或兩情相悅?陸生來台政策之匯流與轉變。**教育研究與發展期刊，6**（2），145-180。

周宛青（2019）。由境外生在臺面對問題反思高等教育國際化策略。**臺灣教育評論月刊，8**（11），7-15。

馬藹萱（2014）。從在臺外籍生之學習選擇看留學生遷移決策之社會建構。**人口學刊，48**，43-94。

陳淑慧、林筱筑、劉騏甄、莊承鉚、劉家誠（2018）。跨國際學生交換環境對來台學習意願之探討——以馬來西亞，菲律賓，越南為例。**環境與管理研究，19**（2），31-60。

張芳全（2017）。東南亞國家學生留學臺灣的經驗與建議之研究。**臺北市立大學學報，48**（2），1-27。

張芳全、余民寧（1999）。亞洲國家與美國間留學互動因素之探索。**教育與心理研究，22**，213-250。

黃庭玫（2019）。**東南亞境外學生來台就讀高等教育之推拉因素與變遷研究：以越南與馬來西亞為例**（未出版博士論文）。國立臺南大學，臺南市。

詹盛如（2017）。亞洲跨境學生流動：哪些品質重要呢？。**評鑑雙月刊，70**，19-21。

溫子欣（2019）。對於國際生在臺就學困難研究的觀察與建議。**臺灣教育評論月刊，8**（11），16-20。

蔡文榮、巫麗芳（2013）。越南籍學生在臺灣的大學適應議題之研究：以中興大學為例。**中臺學報，24**（4），75-96。

蔡文榮、徐主愛（2013）。外籍學生在臺灣的大學適應議題之研究：以中興大學之泰國學生為例。**教育科學期刊，12**（2），82-111。

蔡文榮、石裕惠（2015）。日本籍國際學生在臺灣中部大學適應議題之個案研究。**臺中教育大學學報，29**（2），1-37。

蔡文榮、陳雅屏（2015）。初抵臺灣的印度學生在中興大學適應議題之研究。**教育科學期刊，14**（1），19-56。

潘俊宏、張仁家（2019）。新南向政策背景下國際學生來臺留學現況暨影響因素初探。**臺灣教育評論月刊，8**（2），154-175。

薛家明（2015）。我國招收境外學生之現況與思辨。**高等教育研究紀要，3**，1-19。

Hee, O. C. (2014). Validity and reliability of the customer-oriented behaviour scale in the health tourism hospitals in Malaysia. *International Journal of Caring Sciences*, 7(3), 771-775.

Nghia, T. L. H. (2015). *Factors influencing prospective international students' motivation for overseas study and selection of host countries and institutions: The case of Vietnamese students*. In 26th ISANA International Education Association Conference.

Pham, M. L., Wu, C. L., & Blohm, M. A. (2017). International students' learning satisfaction and its associated factors in Taiwan. **建國科大社會人文期刊, 36**(1), 40-61.

Roberts, A., Chou, P., & Ching, G. (2010). Contemporary trends in East Asian higher education: Dispositions of international students in a Taiwan university. *Higher Education, 59*(2), 149-166.

Thai, T. T. H. (2013). Re-examining push-pull factors in international student flows between Vietnam and Taiwan. *Journal of Thu Dau Mot University, 2*(9), 47-58.

利用UCAN職能資料檢核就業提升之技職教育實務經驗探討
——以虎尾科技大學實施案例

國立虎尾科技大學職涯發展中心
國立虎尾科技大學農業科技系
楊閔惠

壹、研究目的

針對技職教育就業問題：包括缺乏技術職能（硬技能），和求職者經驗不足，缺乏職場職能（軟技能）已成為全球性徵才的問題。學生入學後的學習動機低落、學習行為與成就不如預期，為了降低學用落差，增加學生職場就業力。

由於技職教育招生策略及學生來源多元化，學生所就讀科系與自身的特質和選擇，往往不相契合（王秀槐，2006）。因此造就學生入學後的學習動機低落、學習行為與成就不如預期（王秀槐、黃金俊2010）。2017年教育部亦針對技職教育特舉辦契合式人才培育的論壇，針對德國、韓國、日本、大陸等國人才培育做深入論壇。（教育部，2017）。各國職業教育的特色與分析在學習成效面向，德國、奧地利、瑞士，都以企業培訓為主，職校教育為輔，我國以學校為主，學生投入職場仍需銜接教育。因此，如何規劃一套銜接教育，能夠成功將教育與職場銜接是技職教育須努力的方向。

由於我國產業極需轉型升級，技職教育培育出之技術人才漸漸無法滿足企業所需，如何藉由德國教育體制，理論與實務並重，並將現代專精之大量工業科目列入教育裡，並積極發展學校與企業界的合作機制，讓培育出的學生能接軌產業工業技術與生產。

針對技職教育如何落實學生學用落差的問題。如何提升學生就業力所需具備技術職能與職場職能為當前需要解決的問題。為提升學生的就業接軌最後一哩路，規劃從培育、實習到就業，以創新做法打造契合式產業學院培育具有實做力及就業力之產業所需人才。為落實學生畢業前修習校外實習課程，增進學生實務經驗，縮短學用落差。

建立「UCAN課程地圖」，運用職能具體化系所核心能力、發展課程地圖，以利各系所進行：持續檢視調整系所定位、職涯進路及核心能力、調整課程及教學內容、調整教學資源分配、運用UCAN職能／知識技能進行課程對應盤點、檢視專業職能與課程的雙向對應關係等項目，並提供學生依UCAN就業途徑對應系所職涯進路。進一步，為了強化學生實務技術能力，積極媒合學生校外實習強化專業職能，讓學生就業接軌速度在畢業即就業。

由職涯中心統籌進行施測推動，協助校發中心收集相關IR所需資訊，分析診斷、修改回饋給教學發展中心與各系所需求，藉由各系之課程地圖進行教學檢核，加強相關知識與技能在課程中之比重，以提升各系核心專業職能，減少學用落差。

貳、研究方法

運用UCAN職能／知識技能進行課程對應盤點、檢視專業職能與課程的雙向對應關係，並提供學生依UCAN就業途徑對應系所職涯進路。透過大專校院就業職業平台-UCAN與畢業生流向資料勾稽對應關係。UCAN就業途徑對應職能優勢與課程能量分析。

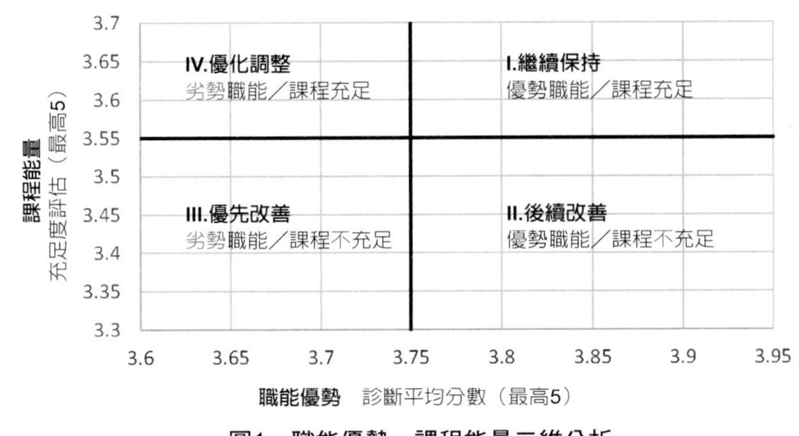

圖1　職能優勢—課程能量二維分析

一、施測對象：

（106-108學年度）日間部四技一至四年級學生。

二、共通職能與專業職能二維分析，探討職能及就業滿意度：

（一）設定二維分析臨界值參考點

由UCAN平台可獲得共通職能與專業職能二維分析結果，分析臨界值參考點為全校平均值、各系平均值或其他設定值。

（二）二維分析分群結果與教學發展比對

二維分析結果可獲得四象限分群建議，與各系核心能力養成目標進行比對，可作為長期追蹤與評估學生職能養成情形參考，提供日後教學發展調整參考資料。

（三）二維分析職能診斷對應課程地圖

透過UCAN二維分析將共通職能、專業職能施測結果進行「職能優勢」與「課程能量」兩項就業力指標分數統計，分群出四個象限，如圖1說明。

透過專業職能問卷學生在系所核心就業途徑診斷情形，系所也可透過二維分析結果了解各就業途徑面向二維分析情形，可作為探討回饋教學端之依據。

參、研究成果與討論

利用UCAN資料檢視專業職能與課程的對應關係，檢核學生學習及學生就業滿意度之探討。檢視虎尾科技大學契合式產業學院對就業提升之助益實務經驗探討。共通與專業職能養成、就業準備情形與對接就業狀況。本研究透過UCAN平台進行相關施測統計，並在專業職能方面對焦66種就業途徑與職業能力面向說明，透過課程地圖比對，探討專業職能及共通職能與本校課程相對應，找出能力面向與課程間之關係，探討課程是否符合系所職能培育方向，以期降低學用落差、提升就業滿意度。每學年辦理畢業生就業滿意度調查，做為課程規劃依據。

本研究之推動施測診斷對象為日間部一至四年級學生，共四個院及20個系所。

表1　推動三學年度之人數及總施測率

日間部四技	總班級人數	職業興趣診斷人數	職場共通職能診斷人數	專業職能診斷人數	總診斷人次	總施測率
106學年	7136	1907	1354	1149	4410	21%
107學年	7137	3057	3189	2198	8444	39%
108學年	6646	4479	5679	5318	15476	78%

註：資料來源由國立虎尾科技大學職涯發展中心統計

一、本校107學年度共通職能與全國平均值比較

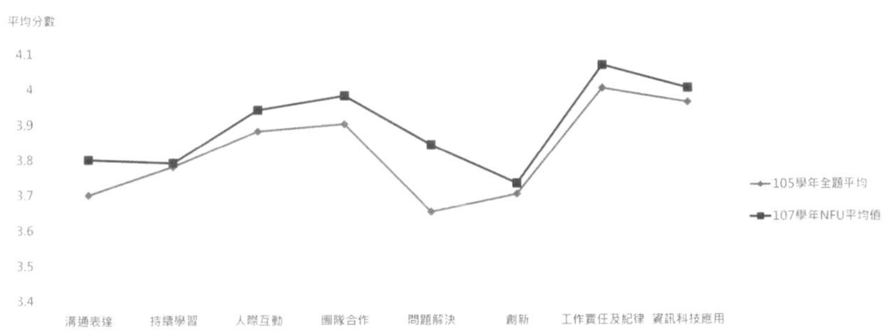

圖2　107學年度共通職能與全國平均值比較（由教育部UCAN辦公室提供）

二、國立虎尾科技大學106-108年共通職能

表2　全校106-108學年共通職能參考值

日間部四技	共通職能平均分數		
	106學年（全部）	107學年（全部）	108學年（全部）
溝通表達	3.80	3.77	3.79
資訊科技應用	4.00	3.98	3.88
工作責任及紀律	4.06	4.08	4.02
創新	3.74	3.70	3.73

日間部四技	共通職能平均分數		
	106學年（全部）	107學年（全部）	108學年（全部）
持續學習	3.79	3.76	3.77
人際互動	3.93	3.92	3.89
團隊合作	3.98	3.98	3.95
問題解決	3.84	3.79	3.82

註：資料來源由國立虎尾科技大學職涯中心整理

虎尾科技大學106-108年全校共通職能表現，由表2 結果顯示：本校學生在團隊合作、人際互動和工作責任及紀律表現較為優異。由圖2 結果顯示：針對問題解決本校表現優於全國。透過教育部UCAN平台的分析診斷結果顯示如表3 108學年全校共通職能分析結果，職能優勢診斷結果表現較佳，在課程能量方面，課程或活動充足度評估有待再提升。二維分析結果顯示，溝通表達及創新為優先改進項目。

表3　108學年全校共通職能二維分析

職場共通職能面向	職能優勢 診斷平均分數	課程能量 課程或活動 充足度評估	二維分析
溝通表達	3.79	3.54	III. 優先改進
持續學習	3.77	3.67	IV.優化調整
人際互動	3.89	3.59	II. 後續改進
團隊合作	3.95	3.76	I. 繼續保持
問題解決	3.82	3.66	IV.優化調整
創新	3.73	3.37	III. 優先改進
工作責任及紀律	4.02	3.74	I. 繼續保持
資訊科技應用	3.88	3.66	I. 繼續保持
平均值	3.86	3.62	

註：1.資料來源由國立虎尾科技大學職涯中心整理
　　2.分數最高5

三、國立虎尾科技大學專業職能診斷

由圖3結果顯示：以本校108學年度工程學院各系診斷人數、職涯類型為例說明，整體來說在工程技術科學相關人數占比最多，其次是製造、物流運輸和資訊科技。透過專業職能問卷，讓學生了解自己在系所核心就業途徑診斷情形，系所也可透過二維分析結果了解各系就業途徑面向，可作為教學課程探討回饋之依據。

以本校108學年度工程學院各系專業職能職涯類型如下：

108學年工程學院與各系專業職能主要職業類型施測分布情形

職涯類型	動力機械(工程)學系	材料科學與工程學系	機械與電腦輔助工程系	機械設計工程系	自動化(控制)工程系	車輛工程(學)系	飛機工程系	工程學院
物流運輸	0	0	0	59**	0	0	27**	86**
科學、技術、工程、數學	64**	223	117	275	284	271	498	1732
製造	13**	93**	62**	0	25**	6**	69**	268**
資訊科技	0	0	0	0	0	0	49**	49**

註：**1. 若施測人數未達該年度全系總數50%以上，統計結果較不具參考價值。

圖3　本校108學年度工程學院各系專業職能職涯類型

表4 108學年度專業職能之工程及技術就業途徑二維分析結果顯示，工程及技術項目可分為三個專業職能面向，分別為瞭解工程以及技術研發流程中所需的相關基本概念和步驟、將應用技術的概念和步驟運用在各領域的問題上以及應用工程實務的專業知識，將研發成果落實於產品之生產及製造上。藉由UCAN專業職能二維分析統計，可以了解到工程學院學生專業職能面向在職能優勢職能診斷平均分數較課程能量系所課程充足程度評估哪些面向表現較佳。進一步藉由各系之課程地圖進行教學檢核，加強相關知識與技能在

課程中之比重，以提升各系核心專業職能，減少學用落差。因此，對於職能優勢及課程能量充足評估，有待進一步盤點課程和課程地圖及學生就業進路類型相呼應，才能有效輔導學生就業選擇。

藉由UCAN平台所建立就業途徑和能力面向如圖5、6內容所示，以自動化系為實施案例說明，其所對應診斷人數、職涯類型、就業途徑及其診斷分數，可以作為教學課程規劃的參考。進一步結合表4 就業途徑二維分析，將專業職能面向在職能優勢職能診斷平均分數和課程能量系所課程充足程度評估，匯整作為教學課程建議的依據和學生就業類型和能力面向評估的參考。

表4　108學年度專業職能之工程及技術就業途徑二維分析結果

職涯類型	就業途徑	專業職能面向	職能優勢職能診斷平均分數（最高5）	課程能量系所課程充足程度評估（最高5）	二維分析
科學、技術、工程、數學	工程及技術	瞭解工程以及技術研發流程中所需的相關基本概念和步驟	3.76	3.72	IV.優化調整
		將應用技術的概念和步驟運用在各領域的問題上。	3.82	3.64	II.後續改進
		應用工程實務的專業知識，將研發成果落實於產品之生產及製造上。	3.76	3.65	III.優先改進
		專業職能面向平均分數	3.78	3.67	
		施測人數	2515人		

註：資料來源由國立虎尾科技大學職涯中心整理

實施案例：以自動化系為例如下：

就業途徑	能力面向
工程及技術	將應用技術的概念和步驟運用在各領域（包含．工程、醫療、農業、生物技術、能源和電力、運輸、資訊通訊、製造和建築）的問題上。
生產管理	在生產的過程中協調工作團隊，以提高製程的績效。
製程研發	在製造流程中執行持續改善的程序，以維持品質

圖4　自動化系就業途徑和能力面向

❑自動化(控制)工程系

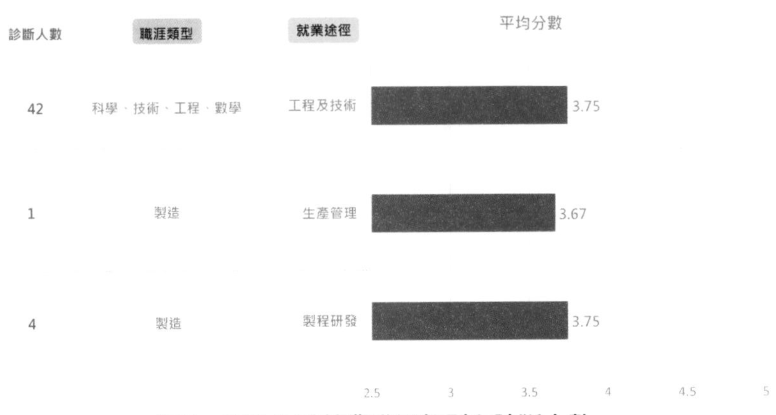

圖5　自動化系就業職涯類型和診斷人數

表5　105-109 學年度畢業滿一年畢業生就業狀況

調查年度	畢業學年度	畢業生人數	完成資料調查人數	完成資料調查%	畢業流向（%）
					就業
105	103	2239	1375	61.41	37.20
106	104	2213	1356	61.27	46.64
107	105	2106	1369	65.10	56.82

調查年度	畢業學年度	畢業生人數	完成資料調查人數	完成資料調查%	畢業流向（%）
					就業
108	106	2149	1365	63.51	57.65
109	107	2059	1443	70.08	58.07

四、契合式產業學院對畢業生實習及就業之提升

105-109學年度畢業滿一年畢業生就業狀況，由畢業生流向就業逐年增加就業百分比如表5，探討本校實習人數在學期及學年實習有增加趨勢，105年共279人，106年共359人，107年共357人。本校自104年建立契合式產業學院共引進1600萬元的企業資金，大幅增加實習及就業的機會。其運作內容包括：引進產官學研資源，與企業建置一運作SOP，雙方並共同建置一平台，藉由計畫資源及企業資金，雙方共同目標以技術研發和人才培育，其目標在於提升企業競爭力。其運作模式雙方共同招募及培育學生，並建置社團活動，社團由業師定期到校上課，採雙導師制一位業界導師和一位校內教師共同規劃，並利用暑假開設工業基礎技術模組課程，由語言中心協助開設德文、義大利文，並進一步規劃國際產業學院，送學生到德國和義大利進行海外實習，強化學生的國際觀。

藉由107學年畢業生流向與最後一年在校共通職能分數勾稽，對應就業狀況。了解學生與產業對接之各種情形，工作狀況對應之共通職能分數，未來可作為在校生職能與就業參考。了解整體學習表現，有助於未來教學做滾動式修正。

由表7所示，進入政府部門之校友有共通職能分數在4分以上，分別為人際互動、團隊合作、問題解決、工作責任及紀律、資訊科技應用，屬於優質學生。其中，自由工作者之校友共通職能分數在4分以上，分別為持續學習、人際互動、團隊合作、創新、工作責

表6　107學年畢業滿一年畢業生在校時於UCAN最後一次共通職能分數

工作狀況	在校時於UCAN最後一次共通職能分數								人數
	溝通表達	持續學習	人際互動	團隊合作	問題解決	創新	工作責任及紀律	資訊科技應用	
	平均數	平均數	平均數	平均數	平均數	平均數	平均數	平均數	
1全時工作	3.73	3.76	3.89	3.92	3.71	3.64	4.04	3.92	450
(1)企業（包括民營企業或國營企業…等）	3.73	3.75	3.87	3.90	3.70	3.63	4.03	3.91	419
(2)政府部門（含職業軍人）	3.85	3.83	4.22	4.23	4.01	3.79	4.27	4.17	16
(3)學校（包括公立及私立大學、高中、高職、國中小…等）	3.71	3.86	3.90	3.94	3.73	3.80	3.97	3.87	5
(4)非營利機構	3.57	3.72	4.09	3.50	3.92	3.00	3.57	3.25	2
(5)創業	3.76	3.76	4.50	4.15	3.78	3.50	4.10	3.67	3
(6)自由工作者（以接案維生或個人服務，例如撰稿人…）	3.46	4.00	4.07	4.03	3.70	4.00	4.32	3.90	5
(7)其他									
2部分工時									
3家管／料理家務者									
4目前非就業中	3.69	3.76	3.82	3.91	3.73	3.66	4.00	3.91	337
(1)升學中或進修中	3.75	3.84	3.88	3.95	3.77	3.73	4.01	3.95	187
(2)服役中或等待服役中	3.71	3.74	3.79	3.92	3.71	3.64	4.07	3.95	54

工作狀況	在校時於UCAN最後一次共通職能分數								人數
	溝通表達	持續學習	人際互動	團隊合作	問題解決	創新	工作責任及紀律	資訊科技應用	
	平均數	平均數	平均數	平均數	平均數	平均數	平均數	平均數	
(3)準備考試	3.58	3.64	3.76	3.89	3.69	3.53	3.99	3.84	47
(4)尋找工作中	3.56	3.54	3.67	3.78	3.63	3.50	3.87	3.76	49
(5)其他：不想找工作、生病…									

註1：畢業生若選擇「1全時工作」，需續填工作機構性質（有7種）

註2：畢業生若選擇「4目前未就業」，需續填未就業原因（有5種）

註3：資料來源由國立虎尾科技大學職涯中心整理

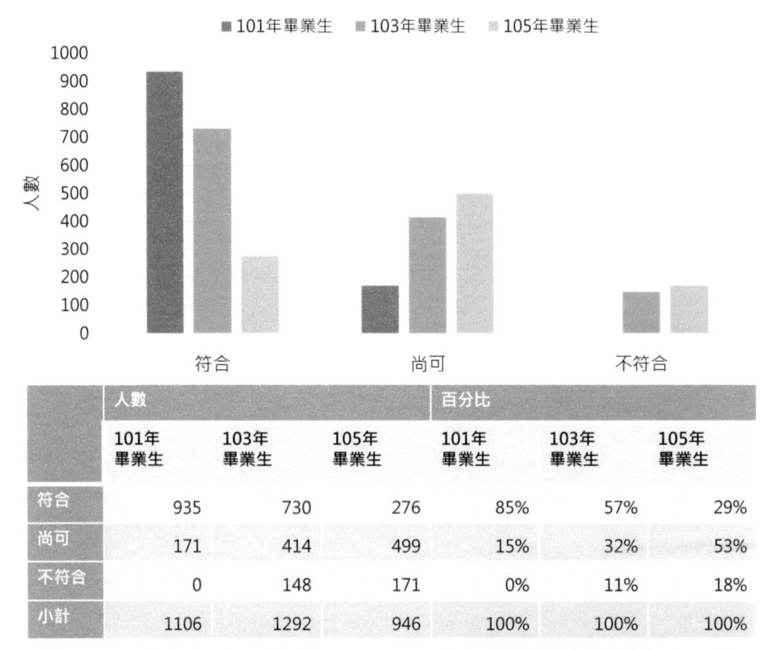

	人數			百分比		
	101年畢業生	103年畢業生	105年畢業生	101年畢業生	103年畢業生	105年畢業生
符合	935	730	276	85%	57%	29%
尚可	171	414	499	15%	32%	53%
不符合	0	148	171	0%	11%	18%
小計	1106	1292	946	100%	100%	100%

圖6　105學年調查畢業滿一、三、五年畢業生對在學滿意度呈現

任及紀律，也屬於優質學生。針對非就業校友尋找工作中所對應八大共通職能表現，普遍較為低落值得進一步探討共通職能與未來就業之關係。

由圖6顯示：105學年調查畢業滿一、三、五 年畢業生對在學所讀系所之專業訓練滿意度呈現，對專業所學與就業符合滿意度，由29%、57%、85%逐年提高；不符合程度幾乎降至0%。

肆、結論

一、105學年調查畢業滿一、三、五年畢業生對在學所讀系所之專業訓練滿意度呈現，對專業所學與就業符合滿意度逐年提高，不符合程度幾乎降至0。

二、藉由107學年畢業生流向與最後一年在校共通職能分數勾稽，對應就業狀況。了解學生與產業對接之各種情形，工作狀況對應之共通職能分數，未來可作為在校生職能與就業參考。了解整體學習表現，有助於未來教學做滾動式修正。

三、在技職教育體系為提升學生的就業接軌最後一哩路，規劃從培育、實習到就業，以創新做法建立契合式產業學院有助於提升學期實習，直接與就業對接提升就業力。

四、由就業途徑二維分析，將專業職能面向在職能優勢職能診斷平均分數和課程能量系所課程充足程度評估，匯整作為教學課程建議的依據和學生就業類型和能力面向評估的參考。未來可進一步盤點課程和課程地圖及學生就業進路類型相呼應，才能有效輔導學生就業選擇。

五、進入政府部門之校友有共通職能分數在4分以上，分別為人際互動、團隊合作、問題解決、工作責任及紀律、資訊科技應用，屬於優質學生。

六、針對非就業校友尋找工作中所對應八大共通職能表現，普遍較為低落值得進一步探討共通職能與未來就業之關係。

七、由職涯中心統籌進行施測推動，協助校發中心收集相關IR所需資訊，分析診斷、修改回饋給教學發展中心與各系所需求，藉由各系之課程地圖進行教學檢核，加強相關知識與技能在課程中之比重，以提升各系核心專業職能，減少學用落差。

伍、預期提供校務發展之具體運用方向

實際執行期間	自109年4月15日起，至109年10月31日止
研究結果之運用（可複選）	□已提供本校校務發展及決策之參考　□預期提供給＿＿＿＿＿＿＿＿單位 □已投稿國內外學術研討會並獲發表　□預計投稿國內外學術研討會 （□國內研討會，會議名稱：＿＿＿＿＿＿＿＿＿，會議日期：＿＿＿＿＿； □國外研討會，會議名稱：＿＿＿＿＿＿＿＿＿，會議日期：＿＿＿＿＿；） □已投稿國內外學術期刊並獲發表　■預計投稿國內外學術期刊 （□國內期刊，期刊名稱：＿＿＿＿＿＿＿＿＿，刊登日期：＿＿＿＿＿； □國外期刊，期刊名稱：＿＿＿＿＿＿＿＿＿，刊登日期：＿＿＿＿＿；） □已指導學生完成學位論文　□已指導學生，但學生學位論文尚未完成 □已指導學生完成專題製作　□已指導學生，但學生專題製作尚未完成

參考文獻

王秀槐、黃金俊（2010）。擇其所愛，愛其所擇：從自我決定理論看大學多元入學制度中學生的科系選擇與學習成果。教育科學研究期刊，55（2），1-27。

潘瑛如、李隆盛、黃藍瑩（2014）。科技大學學生共通職能表現及其對課程地圖的意涵。課程與教學季刊，17（3），39-60。

林宜玄、何敘瑜（2015）。技職教育弱化的隱憂——弱化學生的就業力。臺灣教育評論月刊，4（11），33-41。

感謝虎尾科技大學職涯發展中心提供資料來源

感謝教育部UCAN辦公室及高教深耕計畫提供資源

大學畢業生在專業能耐對職涯滿意的影響：畢業後跨年觀察

輔仁大學學生事務處職涯發展與就業輔導組

壹、前言

學用落差的大學生就業困難議題，一直是各校在教學品保的架構底下，在目標上要極力降低學用落差，這一方面在心理學角度上看見學用落差會帶來心理妥協的心理犧牲，更會帶來長遠的負向影響（蔡秦倫、王思峯，2015），另一方面也暗示了學用落差的降低會帶來較高的職涯滿意。然而理解學生如何度過此類就業困難，則需要觀察兩類角度，其一是觀察前因，學用落差的彌平，抑或是擴大學用落差的可能性，這仍是有待理解的議題，若學用落差持續擴大，那麼帶來的負向傷害可合理的假設會有日益擴大的可能性，學用落差的知覺，亦帶來個體在職業轉換上持續尋求相符合的職業，或是強化自身專業能力的條件，降低學用落差，提高各面向滿意度（蔡秦倫，2016）。

透過蔡秦倫、王思峯（2015）、蔡秦倫（2016）的研究，可見學用落差越低，職涯滿意越高，其立論建構在心理面的妥協，以心理的損傷來描述，然而在Gottfredson和Backer（1981）的理論觀察下，這些心理妥協能持續一段很長的歲月，因此可假設學用落差較高者，除了不滿意持續呈現以外，也感受到翻身無望、轉職困難等挫敗，另外Gottfredson和Backer（1981）雖觀察到心理妥協雖有負向損傷，但在認知失調的情況下，個體會產生正向彌合心理妥協的動力，極力改善較低的社會位置，或是改變既有職業的認知來認同所處的職業身分，然而顯然兩類發展結果的可能性皆有存在的空間，

站在此一問題意識上，在教學品保的機制上，應當將學用落差高、中、低三群體的人，應該有什麼樣不同的預防舉措，這些研究需要仰賴對畢業後的成效進行追蹤與檢驗，方能觀察學習資源的提供，能夠促進個體專業能耐的學習效果，然而在進入職業後如何能延續觀察教學品保的成效，更是較為具有意義的觀察。

另在觀察結果的變化，亦即觀察滿意之間的跨年表現，在職涯發展的過程中，至少涵蓋了三個環節的滿意需要被揭露，首先是校園世界的滿意，這揭露了個體畢業後，有了工作歷練，隨著工作歷練的增加，會回頭評估校園學習經驗帶來的滿意，亦可能從校園的生活滿意，逐漸走向強調學習經驗助益的滿意；至於，工作滿意則可瞭解從畢後一年對工作任務的勝任角度來評估滿意，逐漸走向到工作發展的滿意；最後則是在不同時期皆會挾著對校園端與工作端的評估，而對整體的職業發展的生涯滿意有所評估，特別可以針對此一類型的滿意變化的觀察，來觀察本校學生的職業生涯滿意。

然而揭露此一變化，僅是將專業能耐以及滿意之間的變化進行觀察，進一步本研究所需要揭露的是，專業能耐落差或是相符的不同程度（高、中、低者）會對畢後一、三、五年的負向影響效果為何。在畢業一年、三年、五年的跨時點觀察上，能夠觀察到個體在職業轉換時，生涯選擇、職業跳板的觀念，會不會有機會成為個體內在的認知機制，也是待發現的議題。

因而本文探究本校畢業後學生在轉為工作者之後，跨年度的專業能耐發展的狀況（學用相符高、中、低）進行探究，進一步揭露了職涯滿意、校園滿意、工作滿意的跨年變化，在這些變化上能夠回應較長遠的教學品保上的有效性議題；其次在專業能耐與工作要

求之間的相符程度，又能如何預測畢業一、三、五年的各滿意的表現，實為重要的探究。

貳、文獻回顧

一、學用落差不同視角的差異

在學用落差、高成低就的議題上，一直是大學畢業生就業困難的現象，理解的角度大抵有社會、心理學取向，社會學取向關注在結構性因素造成的社會成因，如產業結構的改變、勞動契約的轉變，來描繪學校端與職業端的技能落差（Allen & Van der Velden, 2001），較不能夠進入個體層面的介入與調整（蔡秦倫，2016）；心理學取向則觀察了學用落差帶來的心理意義，早在蔡秦倫、王思峯（2015）的觀點下，援引了Gottfredson和Backer（1981）的角度，以心理妥協的概念來描述學用落差的心理損傷意義，且關注了心理妥協的後效，意即對職涯滿意的負向影響效果，雖然以個體面的觀點視之，但其揭露了若是遭遇到了學用落差的能耐面的妥協，則會在職涯滿意上有較多的負向影響，然而這些現象不僅阻礙了就業的入職速度，更是會造成個體的經濟滿意、現職的工作滿意、整體職涯滿意較差（蔡秦倫，2016）。進一步蔡秦倫、王思峯（2015）、蔡秦倫（2016）特別觀察了在專業科系內，如工程、會計、法律等科系，較容易受到學用落差的負向影響，而在文理科系內，則較免於學用落差的負向影響，而是較多受到高成低就的負向影響。此外，綜合大學與技職科大亦有差別。

另外，若以教育的觀點來思考學用關係，那麼學用落差則揭示了教學資源以及培養方向與特定的應用環節的落差程度，所以對學用落差程度的介入做法則反映了對教學環境的強化與資源的豐富化，這一點則是在校務經營上非常重要的要點，且若透過學用落差程度的跨時點影響揭露此一現象，則可資源引入以及教學資源優化的期望目標。

二、滿意的貫時表現：校園滿意、工作滿意、職涯滿意

滿意是指個體對所處特定生活事件的評估（Michalos, 1985），而個體在校園世界的知覺、工作世界的知覺，以及職業生涯滿意的知覺，皆會受到生涯發展任務的影響而有所差異，這一點早在Super（1953）認為生涯重視的階段任務是重要的觀察，其認為生涯任務大抵分為五類的任務，例如職業偏好結晶化（14-18歲）是指與自我概念的結合，由教育選擇來進行試探，其次職業偏好具體化（18-21歲），投入某些實作來試探，到了畢業的時期，即為職業偏好實現化（21-24歲），投入一連串訓練與實踐活動，接著，職業偏好穩定化（25-35歲），個體穩定地定錨在特定的職業領域中，最後，職業偏好的傳承化，指的是取得地位與成就。Super（1953）在階段論上，特別在畢業後的年齡上，關注了實現化、穩定化等歷程，可說明畢業後的生涯發展會由技能的關注到職業的穩定化歷程，以此一歷程來觀察畢後一、三、五年的工作與生涯任務的隱含假定的認識。

若結合Gottfredson和Backer（1981）所採用的認知失衡的心理動力以及Super（1953）生涯任務的階段觀點來看，對個體生涯發展來說，畢業後第一年的階段，處於職業的試探期，較容易知覺到校園世界與職業世界的環境差異，當遭遇落差時，應會造成較強烈衝擊，容易對校園滿意度不滿，且可能多歸因於機構面的訓練落差所致；在畢業第三年，處於能耐的發展期，個體的職業發展或許有了職業轉換的經驗，開始關注在個體能耐能夠勝任職業世界要求的知覺評估，當遭遇落差時，容易對工作滿意度不滿，且可能多歸因於個體面的能力落差，不易轉換至理想的職業；在畢業五年後的階

段，處於生涯定錨與衝刺期，個體已經經歷了相關的職業嘗試，能耐的勝任也多少了解自身的發展可能性，正是能夠聚焦職業發展方向並且努力貢獻自己的工作心力與投入，來強化自己的職業價值的階段，當遭遇落差時，容易對工作、整體職涯滿意度不滿，且可能多歸因於個體面的能力落差，不易轉換至理想的職業，也認為整體發展並不是順利的。

校園滿意，是指工作者回顧過去在校園世界中的生活樣貌的心理評估（蔡秦倫，2016），在畢業一年後，多會關心的是校園生活的美好，這是因為工作之後很容易比較出工作生活與校園生活的差異，高於校園世界所培養的專業能耐；在畢業三年後，回顧校園經驗，會開始多關注到校園世界中賦予的技能、知識的充足程度，開始多方充實自身的專業能耐，因而回顧校園世界會較多關注到技能的養成部分，在畢業五年後，則開始焦點在自身的發展與穩定性，回顧校園生活大概會關注在目前的職業發展與科系的專業發展上的對應關係。

工作滿意，是指工作者在工作世界中的樣貌的心理評估（Agho, Mueller, & Price, 1993; Dawis & Lofquist,1984；蔡秦倫，2016），畢業一年多關注到自身職業適應與職業契合的發展，也逐漸關注到工作技能的勝任樣貌來評估自身的工作滿意；畢業三年，則是已經理解個體的專業能耐的勝任情況，多元的專業能耐進修大多也在這些階段會投入更多的心力與關注程度，因而會觀察自身的工作勝任能耐的表現來評估工作滿意，在畢業五年時，則因為職業的定錨發展，對於特定職業群體有高度的認同，因而工作滿意的評估則會是進入該工作帶來的社會聲望或是社會價值的感受。

職涯滿意，則指個體在評估校園端、工作端的整體人生滿意的感受蔡秦倫、王思峯（2015），屬於較為後設評估的層面，在畢業第一年的職涯滿意，大多是關注在校園與工作世界的轉換順利程度來評估職涯滿意程度，畢業第三年後，則多關注到校園世界的專業培養與工作世界的勝任表現等的評估，畢業五年則多關注在校園世界所能提供的職業發展的心理肯認、認同，以及職業發展的定錨效果心理認同概念，因而多以校園、職業的心理認同來思考個體的職涯發展滿意程度。

透過Super（1953）生涯任務的階段任務，揭示了畢業後第一、三、五年的校園、工作、職涯滿意的特殊意義，則可更清晰化滿意概念所代表的背後意涵。

參、研究設計

一、研究架構

本研究欲探究工作所需與專業能耐相符水準，在校園滿意、工作滿意、職涯滿意中的貫時表現，可比較出符合水準程度在這些滿意比較差異。

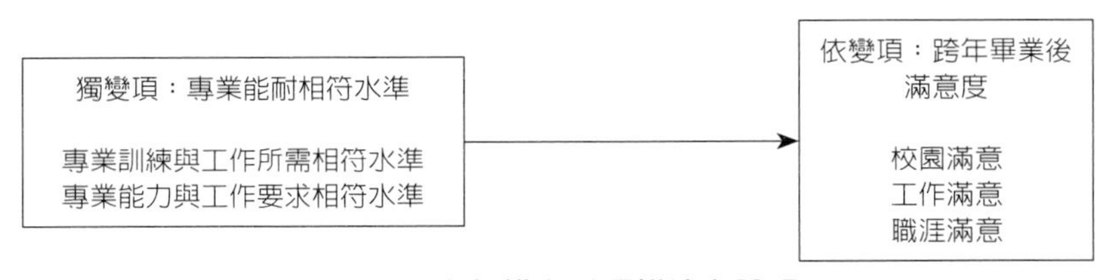

圖1　研究架構與變項描述與說明

本研究觀察個體知覺到機構訓練的學用相符、個體自身能力類別的學用相符變項，對校園、工作、職涯滿意的跨時點變化的差異效果。

本文的主邏輯為學用落差會帶來不滿意，因而假設兩類別的學用相符感受會帶來校園、工作、職涯滿意，且在跨年的資料上可見其趨勢，因而建立假設如下：

H1.專業訓練與工作所需相符度越高，會帶來校園滿意越高。

H2.專業訓練與工作所需相符度越高，會帶來工作滿意越高。

H3.專業訓練與工作所需相符度越高，會帶來職涯滿意越高。

H4.專業能力與工作要求相符度越高，會帶來校園滿意越高。

H5.專業能力與工作要求相符度越高，會帶來工作滿意越高。

H6.專業能力與工作要求相符度越高，會帶來職涯滿意越高。

二、研究對象

研究設計以本校之畢業生之畢業流向調查收集之資料進行分析，以畢業後一、三、五年為跨時資料，資料收集年度由，102學年度到106學年度的畢業後且具有工作身分為樣本，樣本範圍橫跨本校12個學院50科系，全樣本為961筆資料。

三、研究工具

（一）獨變項

專業訓練與工作所需相符。是指個體知覺到所接受的訓練類別與工作所需相符程度，是屬於機構訓練類型知覺的學用相符評估。題項為「您目前的工作內容與原就讀系、所、學位學程之專業訓練課程，其相符程度為何？」，以五點尺度表現，1分非常相符，5分為非常不相符，得分越低，顯示專業訓練與工作所需越是相符。

專業能力與工作要求相符。是指個體知覺到自身所具備的專業能力與工作要求相符程度，是屬於個體能力類型知覺的學用相符評估。題項為「您目前所具備的專業能力與工作所要求的程度之間是？」，以五點尺度表現，1分非常相符，5分為非常不相符，得分越低，顯示專業訓練與工作所需越是相符。

（二）依變項

校園滿意。是指個體評估校園學習生活的滿意程度，題項為「請問您對大學求學經驗的整體滿意度？」，以六點尺度表現，1分非常不滿意，6分為非常滿意，得分越高，顯示對校園學習生活的滿意度越高。

工作滿意。是指個體評估工作生活的滿意程度，題項為「請問您對現在工作的整體滿意度？」，以六點尺度表現，1分非常不滿意，6分為非常滿意，得分越高，顯示對工作生活的滿意度越高。

職涯滿意。是指個體評估橫跨了校園學習生活與工作生活兩端的整體性滿意程度，是以處境轉銜的觀念所能看見的滿意評估，題項為「請問您對職涯發展的滿意度？」，以六點尺度表現，1分非常不滿意，6分為非常滿意，得分越高，顯示對職業生涯的滿意度越高。

四、資料分析方法

不論是在獨變項或是依變項，都觀察了同一個樣本在畢業後一年、三年、五年在相同題項的表現，因而接下來的統計方法，採用了重複量數的統計方法，來觀察其跨年度的趨勢變化。

肆、研究結果

一、畢業後滿意狀態：畢後一、三、五年跨時點變化觀察

首先觀察「校園滿意」之敘述統計，畢後一年平均數為4.70，標準差為 .926；畢後三年平均數為4.67，標準差為 .989；畢後五年平均數為4.68，標準差為1.00。觀察「校園滿意」在球形檢定

Mauchly'W=.993（x2= 9.845，p< .05），達顯著水準，表示跨時點作為受試者內因子違反變異數同質性假設，因此應對檢定所得的F值加以校正，本研究參考Greenhouse-Geisser（G-G）校正自由度作為跨時點之受試者內設計檢定之參考指標（Girden, 1992）。

受試者內之跨時點平均數差異，觀察Greenhouse-Geisser，平均數平方和為.293，F=.537，p>.05，未達顯著水準，顯示雖然校園滿意在畢後第一、三、五年的趨勢尚未達顯著水準，顯示各年趨勢相近，但可見在畢後一年為最高，畢後第三年下滑，在畢業第五年略有回升趨勢。

其次觀察「工作滿意」之敘述統計，畢後一年平均數為4.43，標準差為 .974；畢後三年平均數為4.44，標準差為 1.045；畢後五年平均數為4.51，標準差為 1.038。觀察「工作滿意」在球形檢定Mauchly'W=.991（x2= 12.638，p< .05），達顯著水準，表示跨時點作為受試者內因子違反變異數同質性假設。

受試者內之跨時點平均數差異，觀察Greenhouse-Geisser，平均數平方和為.198，F=.274，p〉.05，未達顯著水準，顯示雖然工作滿意在畢後第一、三、五年的趨勢尚未達顯著水準，但可見在畢後一年、畢後第三年、畢業第五年是逐年上升的趨勢。

最後觀察「職涯滿意」之敘述統計，畢後一年平均數為4.40，標準差為 .939；畢後三年平均數為4.37，標準差為 1.050；畢後五年平均數為4.46，標準差為 1.032。觀察「職涯滿意」在球形檢定Mauchly'W=.995（x2= 7.065，p< .05），達顯著水準，表示跨時點作為受試者內因子違反變異數同質性假設。

受試者內之跨時點平均數差異，觀察Greenhouse-Geisser，平均數平方和為2.666，F=4.019，p<.05，達顯著水準，顯示職涯滿意在畢後第一、三、五年的趨勢，有顯著差異，可見在畢後一年為中高度滿意，畢後第三年下滑，在畢業第五年回升趨勢甚至高於畢業後一年的職涯滿意水準

透過三個滿意度在畢後一、三、五年的調查中，可見校園滿意與職涯滿意有相似的趨勢，兩者都是涉及對過去校園學習經驗的評估，呈現了在畢後一年有中高度滿意，畢後三年滿意度下滑，在畢後五年時有回升的趨勢，在職涯滿意上更是評估了現在工作狀況，因而在畢後五年的職涯滿意度更高於畢業一年後，且整體職涯滿意度，達顯著差異，而在工作滿意度上更是呈現線性上升趨勢，顯示畢業年度越長遠，工作滿意越高。

二、專業能耐知覺：畢後一、三、五年跨時點變化觀察

首先觀察「專業訓練與工作所需相符程度」之敘述統計，畢後一年平均數為1.73，標準差為 1.56；畢後三年平均數為2.09，標準差為 1.45；畢後五年平均數為2.15，標準差為 1.48。觀察「專業訓練與工作所需相符程度」在球形檢定Mauchly'W=.96（χ^2= 60.55，p< .05），達顯著水準，表示跨時點作為受試者內因子違反變異數同質性假設，因此應對檢定所得的F值加以校正，本研究參考Greenhouse-Geisser（G-G）校正自由度作為跨時點之受試者內設計檢定之參考指標（Girden, 1992）。

受試者內之跨時點平均數差異，觀察Greenhouse-Geisser，平均數平方和為75.30，F=51.97，p<.05，達顯著水準，顯示「專業訓練與工作所需相符程度」在畢後第一、三、五年的趨勢，達顯著差異，可見在此類以所接受專業訓練與工作所需的主觀評估上，在畢後一年為最低，然而在畢後第三年的知覺上專業訓練與工作所需的相符程度，立刻攀升，甚至在畢業第五年仍有上升趨勢。

其次觀察「專業能力與工作要求相符程度」之敘述統計，畢後一年平均數為1.49，標準差為 1.20；畢後三年平均數為1.86，標準差為 1.15；畢後五年平均數為1.82，標準差為 1.07。觀察「專業能力與工作要求相符」在球形檢定Mauchly'W=.99（χ^2= 21.08，p<

.05），達顯著水準，表示跨時點作為受試者內因子違反變異數同質性假設。

受試者內之跨時點平均數差異，觀察Greenhouse-Geisser，平均數平方和為58.12，$F=55.05$，$p<.05$，達顯著水準，顯示「專業能力與工作要求相符程度」在畢後第一、三、五年的趨勢，達顯著差異，可見在畢後一年為最低，然而在畢後第三年的知覺上專業能力與工作要求的程度上，立刻攀升，甚至在畢業第五年仍有上升趨勢。

在觀察了專業訓練與工作所需相符程度、專業能力與工作要求相符程度，揭示了在畢後第一年為最低，畢業後第三年以及第五年時，皆會鮮明的上升，顯示學校專業訓練，與自身的能耐培養有相似的趨勢。都在畢業第一年為最低。

三、專業能耐知覺對滿意狀態跨時點變化觀察

進一步觀察到畢業後一年在專業訓練知覺、專業能耐的高中低組別中，在三個滿意向度的知覺趨勢，可進一步探究。首先為求樣本的平均，將原先專業訓練知覺、專業能耐的5點量尺，轉為3點量尺，將得分為1、2分重新編碼為1分，得分3分重新編碼為2分，得分4、5分重新編碼為3分。

首先，觀察在校園滿意度底下，專業訓練與工作相符、專業能耐與工作相符在校園滿意度的跨時點表現。

專業訓練與工作所需相符三區組化效果在校園滿意的畢業後三時點觀察，可見Box'M值為29.80，$F=2.47$， $p=.00<.05$，達顯著水準，顯示三個重複量數的共變數矩陣不均等，而在Mauchly's W值為.99，$p=.04<.05$，達顯著水準，顯示顯示相依樣本違反球形檢定，需要以Greenhouse-Geisser的下限值進行修正，可見專業訓練與工作所需相符，平均數平方和（MS）為15.98，$F(2,958)=9.12$，

p=.00<.05，顯著水準，而三時段未達顯著水準，且專業訓練與工作所需相符X時段，亦未達顯著水準，顯示專業訓練與工作所需相符的三組在畢後三時點之校園滿意度的評估有差異，但畢後三個時點本身無鮮明差異，且交互作用效果亦無差異。

表1　專業訓練與工作所需相符對畢業後三個時點的校園滿意重複量數摘要表

變異來源	平方和（SS）	自由度（df）	平均數平方和（MS）	F	p
專業訓練與工作所需相符（獨立因子）	31.96	2	15.98	9.12	.00
時段（相依因子）	.08	1.00	.08	.08	.78
專業訓練與工作所需相符X時段	2.88	2.00	1.44	1.37	.25
組內	268.84	1916			
受試者間	1678.88	958	1.75		
殘差	1006.96	958	1.05		
全體	5406.59	1921			

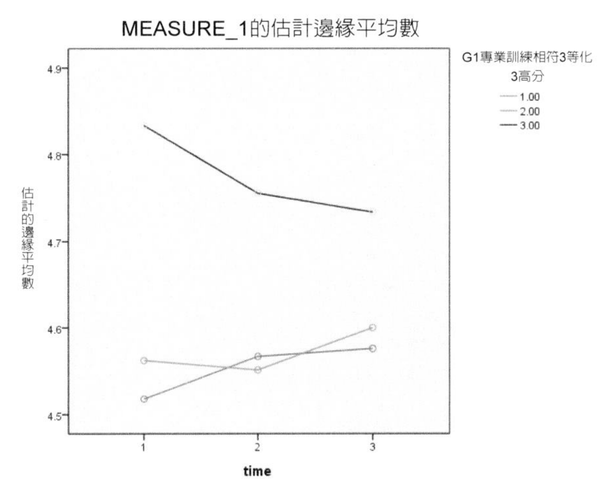

圖2　專業訓練與工作所需相符各水準在校園滿意度三時點的趨勢表現圖

另外，觀察專業能力與工作要求三區組化效果在校園滿意的畢業後三時點觀察，可見Box'M值為18.99，F=1.56， p=.09<.05，未達顯著水準，顯示三個重複量數的共變數矩陣均等，而在Mauchly's W值為.99，p=.03<.05，達顯著水準，顯示相依樣本違反球形檢定，需要以Greenhouse-Geisser的下限值進行修正，可見專業能力與工作要求相符，平均數平方和（MS）為25.74，F（2,958）=14.86，p=.00<.05，顯著水準，而三時段未達顯著水準，且專業能力與工作要求相符X時段，亦未達顯著水準，顯示專業能力與工作要求相符的三組在畢後三時點之校園滿意度的評估有差異，但畢後三個時點本身無鮮明差異，且交互作用效果亦無差異。

表2　專業能力與工作要求相符對畢業後三個時點的校園滿意重複量數摘要表

變異來源	平方和（SS）	自由度（df）	平均數平方和（MS）	F	p
專業能力與工作要求相符（獨立因子）	51.47	2	25.74	14.86	.00
時段（相依因子）	1.15	1.00	1.15	1.09	.30
專業能力與工作要求相符X時段	1.40	2.00	.70	.67	.51
組內	2667.38	1916			
受試者間	1659.00	958	1.73		
殘差	1008.39	958	1.05		
全體	5388.79	1921			

透過校園滿意度來回觀專業訓練、專業能力與工作相符的表現上來看，基本上可見專業訓練、專業能力與工作符合程度的高中低三組，有差異，且可見高分組在畢壹、畢參、畢五皆趨於下滑，但仍是滿意知覺最高，中分組維持平衡一致，而在專業訓練與專業能力上的低分組則有差異，在專業訓練與工作相符上是逐步上升的趨

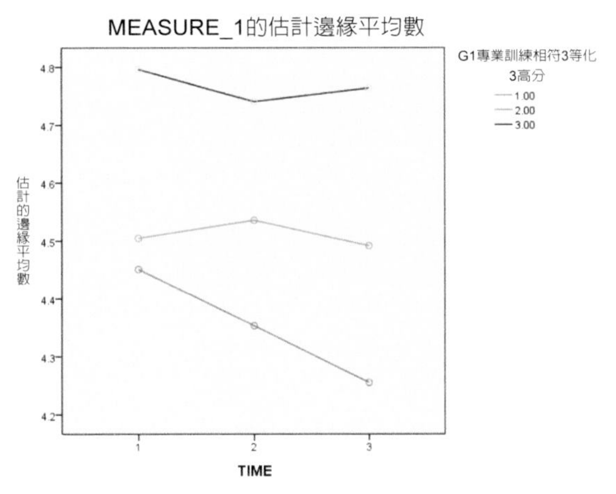

圖3　專業能力與工作要求相符各水準在校園滿意度三時點的趨勢表現圖

勢，相反的專業能力相符上則是下降的趨勢。這彰顯了學校與職場之間的落差仍是存在的，畢業後一年的高分組評估同學，在往後的數年會逐步下修。

其次，觀察工作滿意度底下，專業訓練與工作相符、專業能耐與工作要求在工作滿意度的跨時點表現。

觀察專業訓練與工作所需相符三區組化效果在工作滿意的畢業後三時點觀察，可見Box'M值為30.12，F=2.50， p=.00<.05，達顯著水準，顯示三個重複量數的共變數矩陣不均等，而在Mauchly's W值為.99，p=.01<.05，達顯著水準，顯示相依樣本違反球形檢定，需要以Greenhouse-Geisser的下限值進行修正，可見專業訓練與工作所需相符，平均數平方和（MS）為9.91，F（2,958）=6.150，p=.00<.05，顯著水準，而三時段未達顯著水準，且專業訓練與工作所需相符X時段，亦未達顯著水準，顯示專業訓練與工作所需相符的三組在畢後三時點之工作滿意度的評估有差異，但畢後三個時點本身無鮮明差異，且交互作用效果亦無差異。

表3　專業訓練與工作所需相符對畢業後三個時點的工作滿意重複量數摘要表

變異來源	平方和（*SS*）	自由度（*df*）	平均數平方和（*MS*）	*F*	*p*
專業訓練與工作所需相符（獨立因子）	92.14	2	46.07	30.05	.00
時段（相依因子）	2.09	1.00	2.09	1.57	.21
專業訓練與工作所需相符X時段	5.01	2.00	2.51	1.88	.15
組內	2820.93	1916			
受試者間	1468.85	958	1.53		
殘差	1275.15	958	1.33		
全體	285.67	1921			

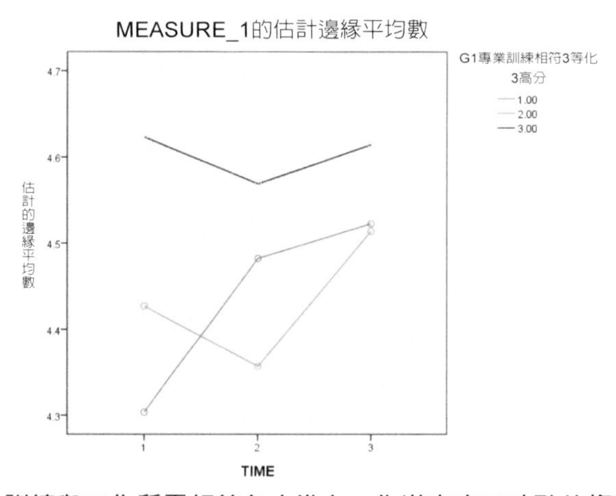

圖4　專業訓練與工作所需相符各水準在工作滿意度三時點的趨勢表現圖

另外，觀察專業能力與工作要求三區組化效果在工作滿意的畢業後三時點觀察，可見Box'M值為44.46，*F*=3.66， *p*=.00<.05，未顯著水準，顯示三個重複量數的共變數矩陣不均等，而在Mauchly's W值為.99，*p*=.00<.05，達顯著水準，顯示顯示相依樣本違反球形檢

定，需要以Greenhouse-Geisser的下限值進行修正，可見專業能力與工作要求相符，平均數平方和（*MS*）為25.74，F（2,958）=14.86，p=.00<.05，顯著水準，而三時段未達顯著水準，且專業能力與工作要求相符X時段，亦未達顯著水準，顯示專業能力與工作要求相符的三組在畢後三時點之工作滿意度的評估有差異，但畢後三個時點本身無鮮明差異，且交互作用效果亦無差異。

表4　專業能力與工作要求相符對畢業後三個時點的工作滿意重複量數摘要表

變異來源	平方和（*SS*）	自由度（*df*）	平均數平方和（*MS*）	*F*	*p*
專業能力與工作要求相符（獨立因子）	51.47	2	25.74	14.86	.00
時段（相依因子）	1.15	1.00	1.15	1.09	.30
專業能力與工作要求相符X時段	1.40	2.00	0.70	.67	.51
組內	2744.00	1916			
受試者間	1659.00	958	1.73		
殘差	1008.39	958	1.05		
全體	2843.24	1921			

透過工作滿意度來回觀專業訓練、專業能力與工作相符的表現上來看，基本上可見專業訓練、專業能力與工作符合程度的高中低三組，有差異，且可見高分組在畢壹、畢參、畢五皆趨於上升，特別在畢業的五年都有上揚趨勢，是工作滿意知覺最高，在中分組、低分組上，專業訓練相符知覺與專業能力相符知覺上則有差異。在專業訓練相符程度知覺上，皆是上升趨勢，但是若進入討論到專業能力相符程度時，則在畢業的三年有上升趨勢，但皆在畢業的五年呈現下滑趨勢。這彰顯了當科系在課程訓練上，會逐漸讓畢業生能夠應用所學，因而工作滿意在不同分組上的知覺，皆是上升趨勢，

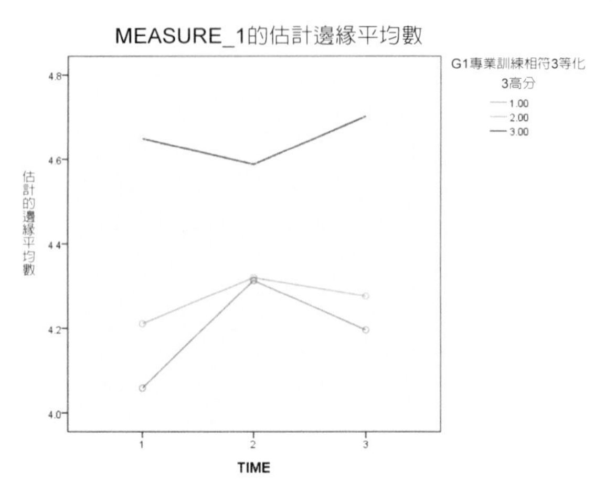

圖5　專業能力與工作要求相符各水準在工作滿意度三時點的趨勢表現圖

然而一旦進入評估個體專業能力相符程度時，除了高分組以外，中、低分組皆會帶來工作較不滿意的情況，因而可見1.工作滿意上的評估，專業訓練相符與專業能力相符的知覺是不一樣的，2.高分組皆呈現工作滿意上揚的表現，顯示學用落差越低工作滿意越高的樣貌，但僅在高分組中可知覺，然而在專業能力越低度相符，則長期會帶來較高的工作不滿意，顯示自身的專業能力上的學用落差越高，工作滿意越差的樣貌。

最後，觀察職涯滿意度底下，專業訓練與工作相符、專業能耐與工作相符在工作滿意度的跨時點表現。

首先觀察專業訓練與工作所需相符三區組化效果在職涯滿意的畢業後三時點觀察，可見Box'M值為14.44，F=1.20，p=.28>.05，未達顯著水準，顯示三個重複量數的共變數矩陣均等，而在Mauchly's W值為.99，p=.14 >.05，未達顯著水準，顯示顯示相依樣本不違反球形檢定，無需要以Greenhouse-Geisser的下限值進行修正，觀察符合球形檢定要求，可見專業訓練與工作所需相符，平均數平方和（MS）為

13.73，$F(2,958)=8.03$，$p=.00<.05$，達顯著水準，而三時段，平均數平方和（*MS*）為3.13，$F(2,958)=4.94$，$p=.00<.05$，達顯著水準，且專業訓練與工作所需相符X時段，未達顯著水準，顯示專業訓練與工作所需相符的三組在畢後三時點之職涯滿意度的評估有差異，畢後三個時點的職涯滿意，亦有鮮明差異，可惜交互作用效果無差異。

表5　專業訓練與工作所需相符對畢業後三個時點的職涯滿意重複量數摘要表

變異來源	平方和（*SS*）	自由度（*df*）	平均數平方和（*MS*）	*F*	*p*
專業訓練與工作所需相符（獨立因子）	27.50	2	13.73	8.03	.00
時段（相依因子）	6.26	2	3.13	4.94	.01
專業訓練與工作所需相符X時段	5.50	4	1.36	2.15	.07
組內	2852.50	1916			
受試者間	1636.88	958	1.710		
殘差	1215.62	958	1.27		
全體	2891.66	1921			

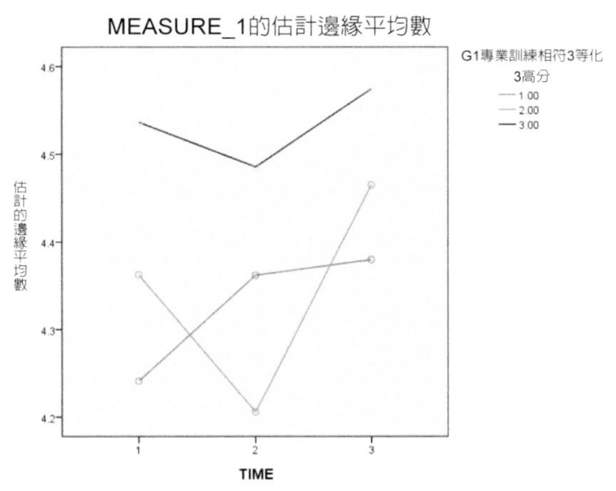

圖6　專業訓練與工作所需相符各水準在職涯滿意度三時點的趨勢表現圖

另外，首先觀察專業能力與工作要求相符三區組化效果在職涯滿意的畢業後三時點觀察，可見Box'M值為27.76，F=2.28，p=.01<.05，未顯著水準，顯示三個重複量數的共變數矩陣不均等，而在Mauchly's W值為.99，p=.16<.05，未達顯著水準，顯示顯示相依樣本不違反球形檢定，不需要以Greenhouse-Geisser的下限值進行修正，觀察符合球形檢定要求，可見專業能力與工作要求相符，平均數平方和（MS）為44.87，F（2,958）=27.42，p=.00<.05，顯著水準，而三時段未達顯著水準，且專業能力與工作要求相符X時段，亦未達顯著水準，顯示專業能力與工作要求相符的三組在畢後三時點之職涯滿意度的評估有差異，但畢後三個時點本身無鮮明差異，且交互作用效果亦無差異。

表6　專業能力與工作要求相符對畢業後三個時點的職涯滿意重複量數摘要表

變異來源	平方和（*SS*）	自由度（*df*）	平均數平方和（*MS*）	*F*	*p*
專業能力與工作要求相符（獨立因子）	89.75	2	44.87	27.42	.00
時段（相依因子）	1.42	2	.71	1.12	.33
專業能力與工作要求相符X時段	2.22	4	.55	.87	.48
組內	2744.00	1916			
受試者間	1567.96	958	1.64		
殘差	1216.07	958	1.27		
全體	2843.24	1921			

透過職涯滿意度來回觀專業訓練、專業能力與工作相符的表現上來看，基本上可見專業訓練、專業能力與工作符合程度的高中低三組，有差異，且可見高分組在畢壹、畢參、畢五皆趨於上升，特別皆在畢業三年時，有略低的感受，但在畢業後五年都有上揚趨

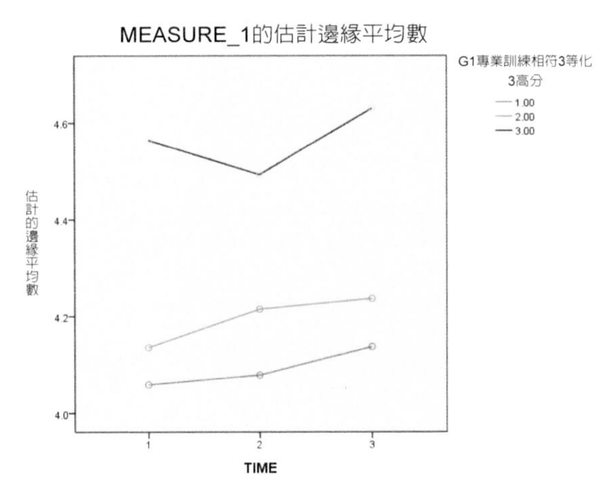

圖7　專業能力與工作要求相符各水準在職涯滿意度三時點的趨勢表現圖

勢，也是職涯滿意知覺最高，在中分組、低分組上，專業訓練相符知覺與專業能力相符知覺上則有差異。在專業能力相符程度知覺上，皆是上升趨勢，頗有學用落差越低，職涯滿意越高趨勢，但是若進入討論到專業訓練相符程度時，則看見中分組與低分組的差異，在中分組會在畢業後第三年有較差的感受，而低分組較不會有較差的職涯滿意感受，會有一路上升的趨勢，而最後皆在畢業的五年呈現上升趨勢。這彰顯了當科系在課程訓練上，會逐漸讓畢業生能夠應用所學，因而職涯滿意雖然在不同分組上的知覺，趨勢有些落差，但是到了畢業後五年的知覺時，都呈現上升的職涯滿意趨勢。

然而若是進入評估個體自我專業能力相符程度時，除了高分組以外，中、低分組皆會帶呈現上升趨勢，因而可見1.職涯滿意上的評估，專業訓練相符與專業能力相符的知覺是不一樣的，2.高分組皆呈現工作滿意皆是上揚的表現，顯示學用落差越低工作滿意越高的樣貌，但僅在高分組中可知覺，然而在專業訓練中度、低度相符知覺的群體中，雖在長期來看仍有較高的職涯滿意，但是在畢業的三年時的職涯滿意較低，特別是中分組的群體，整體長期來講，學用落差越低仍是會有職涯滿意越高的樣貌。

伍、討論與建議

在本校學生的學習成效來看，校園滿意、工作滿意跨三時點（畢業後一、三、五年），雖未有顯著差異，但皆是逐年上升的趨勢；而在職涯滿意上，在畢後第一、三、五年的趨勢則有顯著差異，在畢後一年為中高度滿意，畢後第三年下滑，在畢業第五年回升趨勢，甚至高於畢業後一年的職涯滿意水準。

進一步觀察兩類學用相符類別在三個滿意度上，跨時點的變化。專業訓練與工作所需、專業能力與工作要求的兩個學用相符感受的趨勢線來看，前者較多是評估個體接受科系培養與訓練的課程相符評估，較偏向機構課程相符的學用相符知覺，後者則是多評估自身能力面的相符評估，較偏向個體自身能力相符的學用相符知覺。

若以整體的職涯滿意來看，大抵可見不論是課程相符類型、個體能力相符類型的學用落差，大多可以看見逐年上升的趨勢，雖然在課程相符類型的中分組中較有差異（畢業後第三年會感受到較不滿意），大體皆是上升的趨勢，較符合學用落差較小，滿意會較高的整體假說，但是可見到這僅是在高分組上有穩定的趨勢，在中、低分組上，意旨學用落差較大的的群體，雖仍表現較低的滿意度，但是皆是逐年上升的趨勢。

若細觀工作端的滿意評估，可見在高分組中，不論是專業訓練類型的學用相符，或是專業能力相符的學用落差類型，皆是有較高的滿意度，且逐年上升的趨勢很鮮明，特別觀察到在機構課程訓練類型的學用落差中，雖然中、低分組較低於高分組，但是亦可見上升趨勢，因而這給了本校的課程設計有很高的信心，在課程設計上越是有高的學用相符，整體來講都會帶來畢業後仍有朝向較高的工作滿意，但若評估個體自身能力類型的學用相符，則僅在高分組有上升趨勢，亦即個體若評估個體工作不相符於工作所需時，其工作滿意度會有持平微幅下滑之趨勢。

最後，在對校園滿意的感受與知覺上來說，不論是機構課程類型的學用相符、或是個體能力類型的學用相符感，在跨年的表現上，略顯下滑、趨於中間的趨勢，特別在個體自身能力面的評估相符感越差者，回頭對校園世界的滿意度評估也是較差，僅在高分組上的個體能力相符類型的學用落差，有維持不墜的趨勢。

若將研究回饋至所採的思考觀點，則可見不論是Gottfredson和Backer（1981）所採用的認知失衡的心理動力以及Super（1963）生涯任務的觀點借用，甚至是歸因理論用來理解不同群組的心理評估之歸因，可見在不同時點上，各自有其生涯任務，以內在的心理妥協之彌合動力，不僅回應了Gottfredson和Backer（1981）、Super（1963）觀點的有效意義，也呈現了更創新的理解模式。

本研究回饋至校務經營上來說，機構課程類型的學用相符上來說，若能更加接續工作所需的相符度，雖整體來說會符合學用相符越高，越有較高的職涯滿意、工作滿意，但是在校園滿意則較難以符合此一假設，這或許在畢業生回饋校園生活中，較不容易與機構課程相聯在一起思考，以致於校園滿意會有下滑的趨勢，另外在中、低度機構課程相符上來說，亦有很大的差異，在低分組都有逐年上升的趨勢，然而在中分組，則在畢業後的三年時，會有較差的校園滿意、工作滿意、職涯滿意，這或許是期望機構課程所賦予的環境優勢較高，但因著職業的發展與變化到了第三年正面臨著工作轉換與職涯定錨的議題，因而伴隨著選擇的議題出現時，會較不肯定過去所學的課程內容，使得在畢業的三年時，會較難促進個體滿意，但在畢業後的五年則慢慢回復到不錯的校園、工作、職涯滿意的評估。因而課程設計上可增加職業轉換時的生涯選擇與課程相符的認知。

而在個體能力類型的學用相符評估中，可見高分組有較高的校園、工作、職涯滿意，但是在中低分組則有較低的滿意，且上升幅度僅是微幅，這較符合學用相符與滿意之間的關係組型，但是得注意的是在校園滿意度上，中、低分組的個體能力相符群體，其校園滿意會逐年下滑，是在校園輔導與工作上，需要能夠在學期間多促使個體在遙望未來發展時，不能僅思索一個工作，而是需要思索跨越幾個工作的發展路徑來認知，因而會促進較高的能力相符，故職涯路徑的觀點，職業跳板的觀點，恐怕是重要的介入邏輯，因而可在課程設計上，以職涯路徑角度來思考職業的發展，而非僅關注單一職業的取得議題。

參考文獻

蔡秦倫、王思峯（2015）。職涯妥協的滿意度後效：以學系特徵為調節變項。**中華輔導與諮商學報，48**，1-33。

蔡秦倫（2016）。**機會結構與初職妥協：跨校畢後一年調查分析**。私立天主教輔仁大學心理所博士論文，新北市。取自https://hdl.handle.net/11296/5we56h

Allen, J., & Van der Velden, R. (2001). Educational mismatches versus skill mismatches: effects on wages, job satisfaction, and on-the-job search. *Oxford Economic Papers,53*(3),434-452.

Girden, E. R. (1992). ANOVA: Repeated Measures. Newbury Park, CA: Sage. https://doi.org/10.4135/9781412983419

Gottfredson, L. S., & Becker, H. J. (1981). A challenge to vocational psychology: how important are aspirations in determining male career development? *Journal of vocational behavior, 18*(2), 121-137.

Michalos, A. C. (1985). Multiple discrepancies theory (MDT). *Social Indicators Research, 16*(4), 347-413.

大學招生專業化發展計畫之實施成效與校務治理作為初探

靜宜大學社會企業與文化創意碩士學位學程、
招生專業化辦公室助理教授
沈碩彬

靜宜大學大眾傳播學系教授兼教務長
鄭志文

靜宜大學校務顧問
國立勤益科技大學資訊工程系教授
林家禎

靜宜大學資訊管理學系副教授兼資訊長
葉介山

壹、緒論

台灣自2011年開始形成以繁星推薦、申請入學、考試入學為主的多元升學管道，近幾年「申請入學」名額已逐年攀升，而111學年度大學多元入學方案更以此為主要管道。再者，因應12年國教高中課程架構調整（必修課程數調降、選修課程數調升）、差異化教學與自主學習課程等需求，除了考試入學此一管道之外，高中生之修課歷程與各種學習表現都將會成為大學選才重要參考依據（教育部高教司，2020a）。為了提升考招過程中的公正性、客觀性與系統性，協助審查委員建立更明確的審查標準程序，教育部於2017年開始推動招生專業化發展試辦計畫，第一期（2017年）先邀請申請入學比例較高的大學加入，再逐年擴大邀請範圍，因而第一期有17校加入，第二期（2018年）有30校，第三期（2019年）大幅增加為62校，第四期（2020-2021年）則再新增兩校而有64校加入（教育部高教司，2020b）。教育部期許大學藉由此計畫發展出高品質的專業審查機制，藉以選擇出符合該校系特質與能力的學生。

其次，招生專業化計畫的目標包括：壹、促進大學招生系統化與效率化；貳、落實12年國教新課綱；參、落實國家人培創新政策；肆、促進選才及育才之結合（教育部高教司，2018，2020a）。辦理事項則包括：壹、統整各校／院／系／學位學程之人才培育目標、特色、政策；貳、推動申請入學管道審查機制優化或簡化作為；參、建立招生單位發展、招生專業人才團隊及招生人員培訓機制；肆、結合校務研究（institutional research）與招生改進之專業發展作法；伍、協助經濟或文化不利學生；六、對應111學年度學習準備建議方向；七、推動其他有利招生專業化發展之配套機制與具體作法（教育部高教司，2020a）。

由上可知，該計畫主旨是推動校系申請入學的書審評量尺規（範例如圖1），以求更為客觀與公正地評分與擇才；另一方面，學校須從校務研究角度出發，發展出評量尺規演進與招生策略改進之作法。本校自107學年度開始參與此計畫，已連續四期獲得高額經費肯定，並且成為中區協同主持校之一。本校遂以校務研究思維推動各項配套措施，包括：壹、發展評量尺規並確認有效性；貳、開發評分系統並確認可用性；參、結合校務研究明晰招生成效。以

審查評量尺規（例）

	傑出(90-)	優(80-89)	佳(70-79)	可(60-69)	不佳(-59)
面向一	標準描述				
面向二					
面向三					
面向四					
綜合評語 (Optional)					

註：
1. 面向可為資料類別取向（如修課表現、自傳與學習計畫、校內多元表現、校外多元表現），也可以為能力取向（如學習探索能力、合作領導能力、溝通互動能力、學系專業取向能力）。
2. 校院系可根據審查評量尺規要求審查資料內容與格式，高中端也可從評量尺規了解大學端選才依據。

圖1　書審評量尺規範例

資料來源：劉孟奇（2018）。結合大學選才與高中育才。http://www.kmsh.tn.edu.tw/km107/108-1080525-20min.pdf

下先介紹本校招生專業化的組織架構、資源整合規劃與執行項目，接著再依序闡述實施成效與校務治理作為、校務研究結論與學校對應作法、未來發展。

貳、本校招生專業化的組織架構、資源整合規劃與執行項目

一、組織架構

本校設置「招生專責辦公室」為聯合編組導向，為了提出更有效率、效能之傳遞與回饋，已結合校務研究辦公室之研究能量，

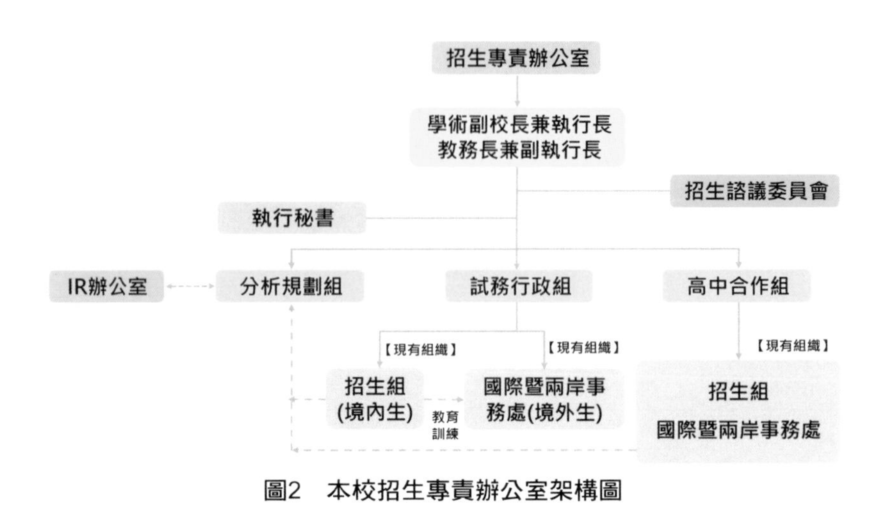

圖2　本校招生專責辦公室架構圖

以因應未來少子化威脅，並與高中攜手合作互動，配合課綱共同育才。招生專責辦公室設有三大組別，各自肩負相關招生事務，其架構如圖2所示。

（一）**分析規劃組**：設有專責教師辦理——1.協助學系建立尺規；2.培訓審查人員；3.執行模擬審查、評分結果分析，及結合校務研究辦公室進行招生策略分析。

（二）**試務行政組**：以現有招生組辦理——1.招生試務工作；2.提供數據。

（三）**高中合作組**：設有專責教師辦理——1.評量尺規對談；2.合作課程，如：共備合授、寒暑輔、優遊台中學、自主學習、戶外教育微專題等。

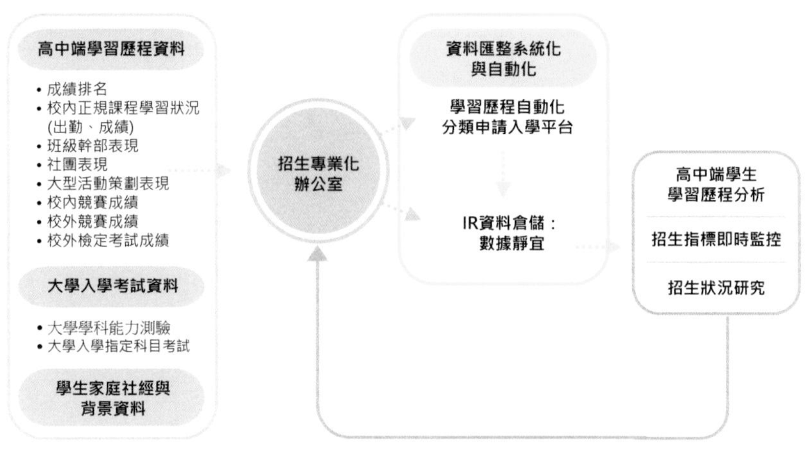

圖3　本校招生議題規劃分析運作圖

二、資源整合規劃

（一）分析規劃面：整合校務研究辦公室、招生組、院系需求與資源

在分析規劃方面，如圖3所示（沈碩彬、鄭志文、林家禎、葉介山，2019）。本校校務研究辦公室與招生專責辦公室合作探究招生議題，如：校務研究辦公室每年就註冊率、就學穩定度等資料繪製圖表，再供招生組瀏覽及分析規劃組討論與分析，以勾勒出本校招生的DNA圖像。基於此，各單位聯繫緊密，共同為招生事宜形成強大支持力。如：有關調升書審比例的理由，需要以校務研究結果與學系溝通，提出有力證明。

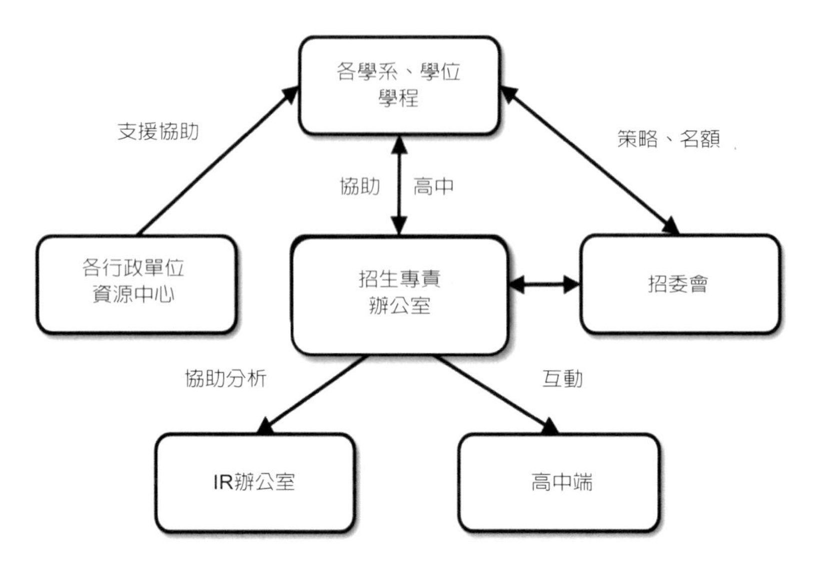

圖4　本校招生事務支持系統

（二）試務行政面：整合如招生組、資訊處等行政單位需求與資源

本校招生試務支持系統如圖4所示，可知招生專責辦公室扮演與各單位溝通的橋樑角色，包括：1.適時引介學系與高中相互進行課程與營隊合作；2.與校務研究辦公室合作，將分析結果與策略建議提供給招生委員會，以作為各項名額與策略調整；3.各行政單位與資源中心均為學系之後勤支援，讓在招生最前端的學系能夠有足夠的多項資源得以使用。在規劃招生專業化事宜方面，力求辦公室永續經營，並且於順利接軌至111學年度後發展為「招生策略辦公室」。基於此，本辦公室在招生試務行政方面，力求結合招生組、資訊處等行政單位的需求與資源，在通力合作的基礎之上，以求招生試務得以順利進行。

（三）高中合作方面：整合學系與高中的需求與資源

本校與高中課程合作方面，一部分由學系自行與高中聯繫，另一部份則由專責教師為媒介，負責協助學系教師與高中聯繫合作事宜。目前合作類型與機制如表1所示：

表1　本校與高中合作類型與機制

高中合作類型	合作機制
1.多元選修課程	主要由本校教師與高中教師共備，由高中教師授課，以協助增能。
2.自主學習課程	（1）本校教師協助擔任學生自主學習計畫的指導教師，如清水高中（楊川欽，2021）。 （2）本校教師前往該校協助某幾週的自主課程。 （3）該校學生於自主學習計畫中之某幾週，搭配外出參與本校教師辦理的活動（可於本校或校外進行）。
3.校訂必修課程	（1）地方學，大致可分為自然與人文兩種。 （2）第二外語，本校可支援西文、日文、韓文。
4.搭配高中各種跨領域學分的課程需求，為高中量身訂做。	

舉例而言，本校於第三期計畫共辦理約30次與高中之「評量尺規與學習歷程檔案」互動，方式包括：互動諮詢、座談會、演講、工作坊、課程介紹等，參與人員包括：校長、副校長、國際長、研發長、各院院長、系主任等壹、二級主管及各學系種子教師等。可知不僅校長帶頭全力支持，而所有教師也逐漸體認到招生專業化的重要性。

三、執行項目

本校招生專業化的執行過程概可分為發展評量尺規、正式書審、評分結果分析等三個階段，如圖5所示，茲闡述各階段重點如下（沈碩彬、林家禎、鄭志文，2019）：

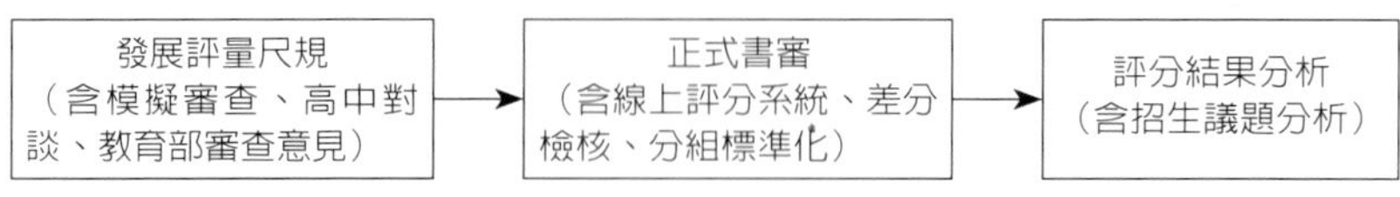

圖5　本校招生專業化的三大執行階段

（一）發展評量尺規

本校在第一期計畫之初有3院12系加入，第二期增為5院17系，第三期再增為6院23系，第四期則全校6院24系投入，請學系設計能力取向的書審評量尺規，而自第二年開始更加作面試評量尺規。評量尺規可以設置如學習表現、問題解決能力、廣域學習能力等能力面向，各能力面向有其占比，且可對應到一至多個審查項目，如：課程學習成果、自傳與學習動機、多元表現等。再者，各能力面向均分為5等第，並設置分數範圍，協助評分更為客觀與公正。

其次，藉由模擬審查協助演練評分過程，自學系隨機抽樣並試評20位前一學年第二階段考生的書審資料，其後進行評分者信度、等第檢核、差分檢核等分析，以獲致評分之有效性為何；再者，學系均辦理與高中對談並且參考教育部審查意見，獲知評量尺規的修正意見，如：1.宜廣泛採計相關學科，不限定過窄科目範圍；2.宜更具體列出標準；3.宜強調反思心得與重視質性課程學習成果。藉由以上作為，學系據以修正評量尺規內容。

（二）正式書審

每年申請入學書審階段，本校藉由線上評分系統，便利審查委員同時輸入等第與成績，並且伴隨等第檢核、差分檢核、分組評分標準化作業、多元擇優等機制，落實專業化評分的規準。其中等第檢核與差分檢核係確認評分委員評選同一位考生的分數差距勿過大，分組評分標準化作業重在協助不同組間考生分數可以比較公正的被比較，多元擇優則是確保在某能力面向突出的考生得以被順利拔擢出來。

（三）評分結果分析

在正式書審後，本校尚會進行單面向等第與分數人數分布、總分人數分布、評分者信度、等第與差分檢核等分析，以供學系修正隔年的評量尺規內容。此外，進行若干招生議題分析，如：1.申請入學生之學測、書審、面試等成績與缺勤、社團、工讀之關聯；2.加入計畫後學系申請入學之註冊率、就學穩定率等情形；3.評分之等第與差分檢核、評分者信度之原理與關聯性探究；4.評分鑑別度與評分者信度之原理與關聯性探究；5.分組評分標準化評分作業之施行與否對評分結果造成的影響；6.本校大一新生入學前後表現之關聯性：大學與高中資料串接調查；7.本校經濟不利與文化不利生之在學相關表現；8.申請入學正、備取生重榜的選擇分析；9.基準大學的註冊率等各項數據比較分析；10.以上各項議題的縱貫研究分析。

承上所述，可知不論是發展評量尺規過程中的模擬審查、正式書審各項機制及評分結果分析，在在均需要執行者具有校務研究的專業思維與能力。因此，本文欲藉以下三點闡述本校招生專業化的實施成效與校務治理作為：壹、發展評量尺規並確認有效性；貳、開發評分系統並確認可用性；參、結合校務研究明晰招生成效。

參、實施成效與校務治理作為

一、發展評量尺規並確認有效性

如前所述，發展評量尺規過程會進行模擬審查並參考高中及教育部審查意見，這些都是以事證為本（evidenced-based）的校務研究作法。以下闡述模擬審查過程所用的分析項目：

（一）評分者信度：

針對「評分分數」進行組內相關係數（intraclass correlation coefficient, ICC）分析，並根據需要採取二因子隨機模型或一致性類型，指標是以ICC值有無達 .40為門檻值（Cicchetti, 1994），藉以確保審查委員間對考生資料評比結果具有一致性。

（二）單面向等第檢核：

針對某一考生資料的單面向所評等級，彼此落差不得超過一等第（賴信宏，2019），此項檢核標準在確保審查委員間對評量尺規等第的見解不致差距過大。

（三）總分差分檢核：

所有委員針對某一考生資料所評總分，彼此差距在7 分以下，此項檢核標準在確保審查委員間對同一考生資料的總分評比不致差距過大（賴信宏，2019）。

模擬審查是否對正式審查時達成各項標準有所助益？如表2為109學年度模擬與正式審查各項分析結果摘錄表，可知絕大多數學系經過模擬審查後，各項指標均有所改善，惟仍有部分未達標準。因此，模擬審查有助正式審查作業進行，有效達成各項檢核標準，從而可確認學系評量尺規之可用性。

表2　模擬審查與正式審查之各項分析結果摘錄表（109學年度）

學院	學系	評分者信度		等第檢核（不合格數）		差分檢核（不合格數）		正式審查有進步嗎	是否部分仍未達標
		模擬	正式	模擬	正式	模擬	正式		
A	A1	.07	.59~.80	1	0	3	0	✓	
	A2	.74	.60~.93	5	0	3	0	✓	
	A3	.01	.76	19	0	17	0	✓	

學院	學系	評分者信度		等第檢核（不合格數）		差分檢核（不合格數）		正式審查有進步嗎	是否部分仍未達標
		模擬	正式	模擬	正式	模擬	正式		
B	B1	.16	.33~.59	10	0	11	0	✓	△
	B2	.17	.99	11	0	10	0	✓	
	B3	.52	.72~.81	4	0	9	0	✓	
	B4	.17	.16~.76	2	0	1	0	✓	△
	B5	.27	.85~.89	14	0	10	0	✓	
	B6	.65	.59~.87	9	0	8	0	✓	
C	C1	.62	.75~.80	16	0	18	0	✓	
	C2	.38	.95	3	0	3	0	✓	
	C3	.36	.59	1	3	5	3	✓	
	C4	.96	.33~.69	2	0	0	0	✓	△
	C5	.71	.90~.94	9	0	5	0	✓	
D	D1	.37	.75	12	0	8	0	✓	
	D2	.64	.86	2	0	2	0	✓	
	D3	.13	.55~.74	18	43	13	0	✓	△
	D4	.15	.28~.55	14	88	9	0	✓	△
	D5	.40	.80	14	0	3	0	✓	
E	E1	.29	.59~.94	15	0	20	0	✓	
	E2	.23	.33	2	0	5	0	✓	△
	E3	.57	.11~.69	4	0	9	0	✓	△
F	F1	.24	.91	15	0	10	0	✓	
	F2	.11	.80	6	0	8	0	✓	

註：1.正式審查因部分學系有分組評分，因而表格內標註學系所有組別ICC值的範圍。
2.正式審查有無進步：ICC值是否提升、等第或差分檢核不合格數是否減少，若有即打✓。
3.是否部分仍未達標：ICC是否部分仍未達 .40、等第或差分檢核是否仍有不合格數，若有即打△。

二、開發評分系統並確認可用性

本校自第二期開發線上書審評分系統，第三期再與資訊處合作優化系統，第四期再整合書審及口試評分系統，如圖6為各期評分方式之演進。茲就第四期系統功能說明如下：

1. **書審及面試均可看見學系評量尺規內容、等第分數範圍及有列印功能（如圖 7）**
2. **依據考生資料評比等第，系統自動設定該等第對應成績範圍（如圖8）**
3. **具有多元擇優功能：**若審查委員認為某考生於某能力項目特優，可勾選擇優。當某生同時被兩位教師點選擇優時，學系可進而討論是否調整評分權重以增加錄取機會，如圖9。

觀光事業學系107學年度個人申請書審資料評分表

考生姓名	專業學習面向(40%)【高中在校成績】					能力特質(20%)【自傳(學生自述)】					多元活動表現(40%)【其他(有利證明)】					合計
	☐傑出	☐優良	☐佳	☑尚可	☐不佳	☐傑出	☐優良	☑佳	☐尚可	☐不佳	☐傑出	☐優良	☐佳	☑尚可	☐不佳	83
	(40-39)	(38-37)	(36-35)	(34-33)	(32-0)	(20-19)	(18-17)	(16-15)	(14-13)	(12-0)	(40-39)	(38-37)	(36-35)	(34-33)	(32-0)	
	34					15					34					
	☐傑出	☐優良	☐佳	☑尚可	☐不佳	☐傑出	☑優良	☐佳	☐尚可	☐不佳	☐傑出	☑優良	☐佳	☐尚可	☐不佳	88
	(40-39)	(38-37)	(36-35)	(34-33)	(32-0)	(20-19)	(18-17)	(16-15)	(14-13)	(12-0)	(40-39)	(38-37)	(36-35)	(34-33)	(32-0)	
	34					17					37					
	☐傑出	☐優良	☐佳	☐尚可	☑不佳	☐傑出	☐優良	☑佳	☐尚可	☐不佳	☐傑出	☐優良	☐佳	☑尚可	☐不佳	79
	(40-39)	(38-37)	(36-35)	(34-33)	(32-0)	(20-19)	(18-17)	(16-15)	(14-13)	(12-0)	(40-39)	(38-37)	(36-35)	(34-33)	(32-0)	
	31					15					33					
	☐傑出	☐優良	☐佳	☑尚可	☐不佳	☐傑出	☑優良	☐佳	☐尚可	☐不佳	☐傑出	☑優良	☐佳	☐尚可	☐不佳	88
	(40-39)	(38-37)	(36-35)	(34-33)	(32-0)	(20-19)	(18-17)	(16-15)	(14-13)	(12-0)	(40-39)	(38-37)	(36-35)	(34-33)	(32-0)	
	34					17					37					
	☐傑出	☐優良	☐佳	☑尚可	☐不佳	☐傑出	☐優良	☑佳	☐尚可	☐不佳	☐傑出	☐優良	☐佳	☑尚可	☐不佳	82
	(40-39)	(38-37)	(36-35)	(34-33)	(32-0)	(20-19)	(18-17)	(16-15)	(14-13)	(12-0)	(40-39)	(38-37)	(36-35)	(34-33)	(32-0)	
	33					15					34					
	☐傑出	☐優良	☐佳	☐尚可	☑不佳	☐傑出	☐優良	☐佳	☑尚可	☐不佳	☐傑出	☐優良	☐佳	☑尚可	☐不佳	80
	(40-39)	(38-37)	(36-35)	(34-33)	(32-0)	(20-19)	(18-17)	(16-15)	(14-13)	(12-0)	(40-39)	(38-37)	(36-35)	(34-33)	(32-0)	
	32					14					34					
	☐傑出	☐優良	☐佳	☐尚可	☑不佳	☐傑出	☐優良	☐佳	☑尚可	☐不佳	☐傑出	☐優良	☐佳	☐尚可	☑不佳	77
	(40-39)	(38-37)	(36-35)	(34-33)	(32-0)	(20-19)	(18-17)	(16-15)	(14-13)	(12-0)	(40-39)	(38-37)	(36-35)	(34-33)	(32-0)	
	32					13					32					
	☐傑出	☐優良	☐佳	☐尚可	☑不佳	☐傑出	☐優良	☐佳	☐尚可	☑不佳	☐傑出	☐優良	☐佳	☐尚可	☑不佳	74
	(40-39)	(38-37)	(36-35)	(34-33)	(32-0)	(20-19)	(18-17)	(16-15)	(14-13)	(12-0)	(40-39)	(38-37)	(36-35)	(34-33)	(32-0)	

第一期：紙本評分，評完要再輸入電腦中

140.128.8.232 顯示

確定

姓名						能力特質(40) 自傳(有利資料、自傳及讀書計畫)					合計
	○傑出	●優良					○優良	○佳	○尚可	○不佳	81
	60-54	53-				6	35-31	30-26	25-21	20-16	
								33			
	○傑出	○優良	○佳	●尚可	○不佳	○傑出	●優良	○佳	○尚可	○不佳	65
	60-54	53-47	46-40	39-33	32-26	40-36	35-31	30-26	25-21	20-16	
			33					32			
	○傑出	○優良	○佳	●尚可	○不佳	○傑出	●優良	○佳	○尚可	○不佳	68
	60-54	53-47	46-40	39-33	32-26	40-36	35-31	30-26	25-21	20-16	
			35					33			
	○傑出	○優良	●佳	○尚可	○不佳	○傑出	●優良	○佳	○尚可	○不佳	76
	60-54	53-47	46-40	39-33	32-26	40-36	35-31	30-26	25-21	20-16	
			44					32			
	○傑出	○優良	○佳	●尚可	○不佳	○傑出	○優良	●佳	○尚可	○不佳	63
	60-54	53-47	46-40	39-33	32-26	40-36	35-31	30-26	25-21	20-16	
			33					30			
	○傑出	○優良	○佳	○尚可	●不佳	○傑出	○優良	○佳	●尚可	○不佳	52
	60-54	53-47	46-40	39-33	32-26	40-36	35-31	30-26	25-21	20-16	
			27					25			
	○傑出	○優良	○佳	●尚可	○不佳	○傑出	○優良	○佳	○尚可	○不佳	71
	60-54	53-47	46-40	39-33	32-26	40-36	35-31	30-26	25-21	20-16	
			35					33			

第二期：初版線上評分系統評分介面

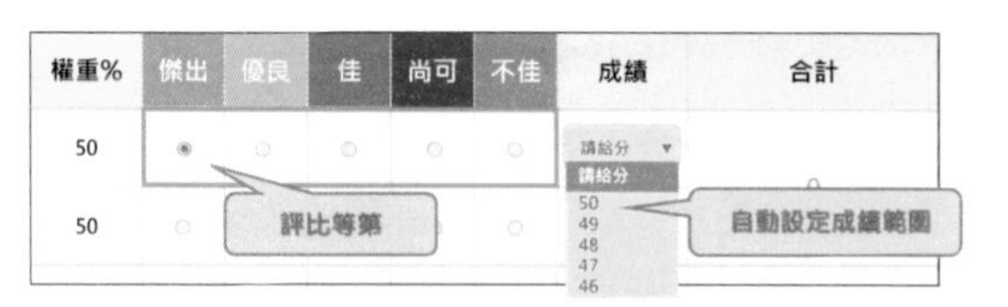

第三期：再版線上評分系統評分介面

輸入面試成績

面試序號	應試號碼	考生姓名	總分	聽力理解 (25-15%)	文法 (25-15%)	發音、口語流利程度與內容 (50-30%)	備註	缺考
1-A-1			88.00	23	20	45		☐
1-A-5			81.00	23	18	40		☐
1-A-9			84.00	22	19	43		☐

第四期：整合書審及面試系統的評分介面

圖6　本校各期評分方式的演進圖

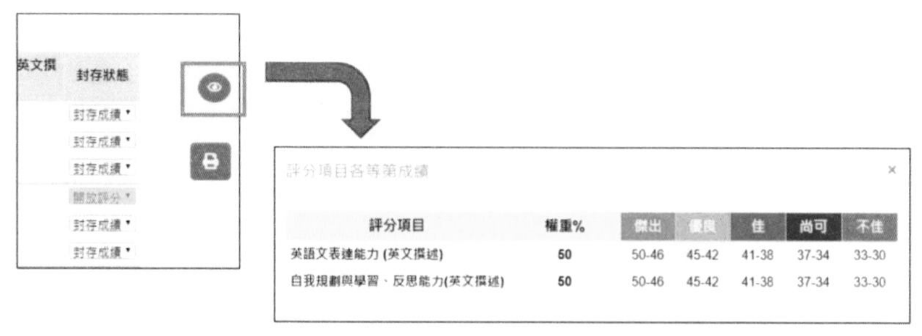

圖7　線上評分系統：點選圖示觀看評分範圍

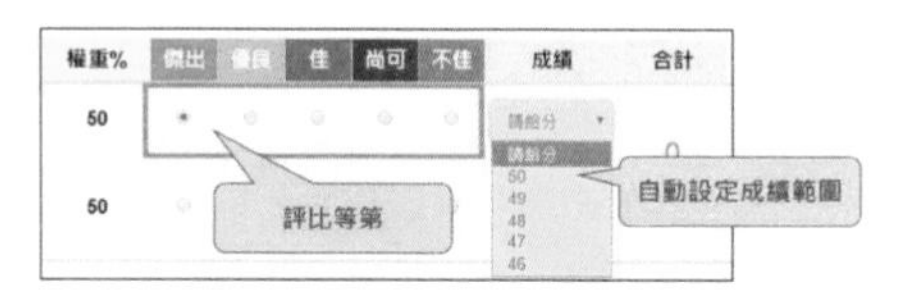

圖8　線上評分系統：
等第對應成績範圍

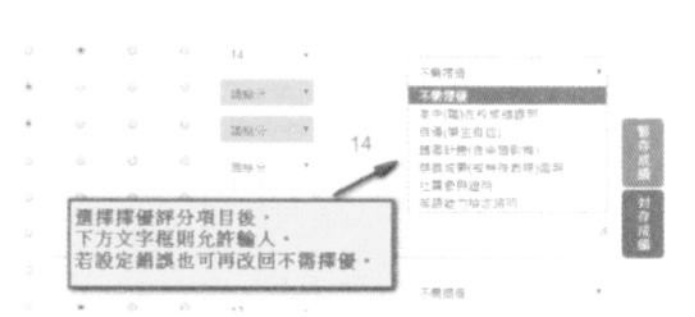

圖9　線上評分系統：
與多元擇優

4. 單面向等第檢核、總分差分檢核、分組評分標準化功能（如前所述）

在正式審查後，本校會蒐集學系使用系統心得，如表3為第三期收集意見，本校據以優化第四期系統，新增如下功能：（1）新增面試評分功能；（2）差分檢核與等第檢核，可一次開放修改成績；（3）書審單項0分或加總超過95分者，增加欄位以說明原因。

表3　學系對第三期評分系統的使用意見摘要表

項目	學系回饋
優點	1. 點選應考號碼可展開PDF視窗 2. 查看評分項目與設定權重 3. 成績欄位以不同底色提示評分狀態 4. 成績欄位透過等第自動設定給分範圍 5. 多元擇優、等第檢核、差分檢核、分組成績標準化、清空學生成績、封存成績、可點選眼睛圖示查看成績範圍、系統美觀、操作簡易
缺點及期待功能	1. 差分檢核與等第檢核：目前需逐筆點選開放，是否可一次開放修改成績？或一鍵自動化處理。 2. 加入自動化摘要提示功能，如：是否曾任幹部、社團、競賽獲獎、證照及其種類、專題成果、語文檢定成績等，並標註佐證符合與否。另外，高中成績之班排百分比亦建議可醒目提示。 3. 用1~5 表示級距，用視窗捲簾點選，再點選成績，可節省頁面。 4. 摘要圖示、成績排序、導出excel表：如各委員評分及總成績平均分布圖，可幫助審查委員檢查差分、分數是否合理。 5. 系統似乎仍有小問題，列印時有遇到分組的表頭與內容資料不一致。 6. 在經過差分、等第檢核後，可否僅顯示哪些考生資料未封存。 7. 書審單項0分或加總超過95分者，可增加欄位以說明原因。 8. 開放承辦人員及系所主管考生備審資料權限。 9. 在異動分數後，遊標自動回到修改處。 10. 頁面顯示：如成績欄位、個人資料、考生編號（序號）於各項功能應一致，以方便檢核作業。

三、結合校務研究明晰招生成效

如前所述，本校已羅列諸項招生研究議題，茲擇取其中兩項分析過程與結果，述之如下：

表4　學測、書審、口試等分數與正備取之關聯摘要表（109學年度）

學院	人數	占二階段比例（%）			學測 vs. 正備取	書審 vs. 正備取	口試 vs. 正備取
		學測	書審	面試			
A	421	50	20	30	.69***	.13*	.46***
B	754	40~50	20~25	25~40	.37***	.26***	.43***
C	661	40~50	10~20	30~50	.35***	.25***	.52***
D	1151	50	15~25	25~30	.45***	.21***	.35***
E	573	50	20~25	25~30	.47***	.13**	.37***
F	83	40~50	20	30~40	-.12	.44***	.74***
整體	3643	40~50	10~25	25~50	.34***	.29***	.36***

*p<.05. **p<.01. ***p<.001.

（一）學測、書審、面試對錄取結果的決策力

為呈現簡明結果，以下僅以學院為單位進行計算，校內則會提供以學系為單位的分析結果，以供擬定招生簡章內容參考。茲計算109學年度申請入學之學測、書審、口試等成績與錄取結果（正備取）之點二系列相關值（正取為 1、備取為 0），分析結果如表4所示（沈碩彬，2020a）。可知多數學院以學測或面試兩者之一，與正取或備取的相關係數較高；且皆以書審與是否正取的相關最弱，此象徵書審比例相對較低，也因此影響書審對錄取結果的決策力。本校據以調升110學年書審比例，A學院調升為20%~25%，B學院為20%~30%，C學院為20%~30%，D學院為20%~30%，E學院為25%~30%，F學院為30%，整體為20%~30%。期許在教育部招生專業化的帶領與推動下，學系對書審作業的決策品質更有信心，以此來預備111學年度學習歷程檔案審查項目的評比。

（二）不同入學管道的在校表現

此項議題雖然為招生校務研究的必要議題，然而，若串聯高中生學習歷程檔案項目，更能明晰在校生學習軌跡（沈碩彬，

表5　主要入學管道學生的大學表現摘要表（107學年）

入學管道＼大學表現	N	高中校PR值		107系PR值		108系PR值		休學率		退學率	
		M	SD	M	SD	M	SD	M	SD	M	SD
繁星推薦	331	70.60	14.53	65.90	25.74	65.41	25.53	0.05	0.22	0.09	0.29
申請入學	1053	38.26	21.78	44.62	26.80	46.13	27.19	0.07	0.26	0.11	0.32
指考分發	758	39.72	23.69	47.67	26.85	48.11	27.04	0.10	0.30	0.16	0.37
平均差異檢定		$F=223.31^{***}$ A>B.C		$F=48.36^{***}$ A>B.C		$F=36.12^{***}$ A>B.C		$F=4.82^{**}$ C>A.B		$F=7.16^{***}$ C>A.B	

$^{**}p<.01$ $^{***}p<.001$

註：本校110學年前另有「類繁星」管道，亦屬申請入學其中一組，報考資格為高中校排前50%，但免書審、面試，本表所列之申請入學則為「一般組」，考生並無類繁星之高中校排限制，且第二階段仍需參加書審及面試。

2020b）。在此以107學年入學生為例，串接高中成績校PR值〔算式：（N-A）/N×100, N為人數，A為名次〕，以及大一、二連續兩學年學業成績系PR值、休退學率，結果如表5。可知不論高中成績、大學兩學年成績，皆以繁星推薦管道入學生最高，申請入學、指考分發管道入學生的高中成績表現則是平分秋色；休、退學率均以指考分發管道入學生略為較多。因此，本校107學年的繁星推薦管道入學生其高中成績、大學成績及休退學率均較佳，申請入學管道入學生則有較低的休退學率，指考分發管道入學生其高中成績、大學成績及休退學率均較為弱勢。此項結果有助我校再發展更為具體的招生策略，例如：若加以計算申請入學管道之正備取生報到率及在學表現，可發現本校以備取生報到居多，且正取生大學成績通常優於備取生（沈碩彬，2020a）；因此，宜設法吸引更多正取生前來報到，以助提升在學生在校表現水準。

表7　正式審查分析結果與對應作法（第三期）

正式審查分析項目	分析結果摘要	對應作法
1.單面向等第人數	部分委員評分分布特殊	宜加強正式審查前委員共識會議
2.單面向分數人數	各組間評分仍寬嚴差距	必要採取分組評分標準化作業
3.總分人數分布	少數學系分數較為集中	宜正視並加強評分鑑別度
4.評分者信度	少數學系評分者信度較低	宜加強正式審查前委員共識會議
5.單面向等第檢核	極少學系未及時修正分數	及早宣布評分措施以利學系預備
6.總分差分檢核	所有學系均符合標準	持續實施

肆、校務研究結論與學校對應作法

一、學系評量尺規之評分者信度、差分檢核數據逐年進步，且模擬審查對正式審查有所助益

本校在分析並綜整正式審查後的單面向等第人數、單面向分數人數、總分人數分布、評分者信度、單面向等第檢核、總分差分檢核等結果後，發現學系隨著經驗積累，各項數據逐年進步，且試評過後正式審查之各項數據均有所改善，惟仍有部分學系之數據未臻理想。茲羅列第三期校務研究分析事證與對應作法如表7所示，所列各項均於第四期加以改善。

二、評分系統滿足學系功能評估，且經試做、壓力、滿意度評估後確認可用性

本校於第三期結合校務研究與資訊處合作開發線上評分系統，在開發系統前蒐集學系功能評估，學系則是經由工作坊、模擬審查試作經驗熟悉系統操作，最後通過系統同時上線人數的壓力測試後，讓系統正式上線。正式審查後，經50位審查委員或秘書回覆

後，針對系統美觀、操作簡易度均給予平均高於8.5分的評價（滿分為10分），且僅1~2位給予低於5分的評價，又本系統衍生論文獲台灣網際網路研討會優秀論文獎肯定（蘇偉順、沈碩彬、葉介山、林家禎、鄭志文，2020）。本校亦根據學系對整體招生專業化流程及評分系統提供建議，成功開發第四期書審與面試整合系統，如表8所示：

表8　評分系統回饋建議與優化作法（第三期）

第三期學系回饋建議	第四期對應作法
1. 開發面試系統	1. 整合書審與面試系統
2. 多元擇優、弱勢生評分措施的預備度不足	2. 將多元擇優與弱勢分的資料評比詳列於評量尺規
3. 等第與差分檢核，建議一次開放修改成績	3. 一次開放修改成績
4. 自動畫出成績平均分布圖，有助檢查差分	4. 增加評分結果統計圖表，供學系即時了解
5. 書審分數異常者，可增加欄位以說明原因	5. 書審單項0分或加總超過95分者，增加欄位以說明原因

三、招生議題分析可回饋本校招生專業化及招生之成效

本校規劃多項招生相關議題，因篇幅所限僅列三項說明結果與對應作法，如表9所示：

表9　招生議題分析與對應作法舉隅

分析項目	分析結果摘要	對應作法
1. 學測、書審、面試對錄取結果的決策力	絕大多數學系，是否正取與學測成績關聯程度最高、面試成績次之、書審成績最低	為提升書審擇才決策力，已於第四期全面提升書審占比

分析項目	分析結果摘要	對應作法
2. 不同入學管道的在校表現	普遍而言，以繁星推薦管道入學生成績最高，申請入學生有較低休退學率，指考分發生其高中成績、大學成績及休退學率均較為弱勢。	1. 確認後續課業成績瞭解恆毅力 2. 積極爭取申請入學正取生報到

伍、未來發展

綜合前述各項說明，本校以校務研究中以事證為本的思維，推動招生專業化各項措施。最後，藉由如下三項闡述招生專業化的未來發展。

一、專業化審查是各校重中之重，可從書審漸次發展到口試或其他招生管道

本校務求全校逐漸投入招生專業化，第一期有3院12系加入，第二期增為5院17系，1第三期增為6院23系，第四期全校6院24系皆投入招生專業化。其次，為推行種種措施，自第一期開始發展書審評量尺規，第二期開始發展面試評量尺規，第三期再從原先單資料參採取向轉型為多資料參採的能力取向評量尺規，並展開弱勢生評分、多元擇優評分等措施。再者，經與高中端討論、參考教育部審查意見、模擬審查、正式審查等階段，各項檢核數據均大幅改善。在未來發展方面，本校藉校務研究成果，第四期參與學系已全數將書審占比增加到20%以上，且多數達到30%，並全校推動面試評量尺規，及規劃原住民專班評量尺規，足見事證為本的校務研究精神大大發揮其果效與價值。

二、評分系統有助教師評分之系統性與便利性，可擴及口試並整合學習歷程檔案評分系統

本校開發線上評分系統，系統功能包括：單面向等第檢核、總分差分檢核、多元擇優等功能，大致獲得學系肯定，但依據學系回饋知仍有需優化之處。因而第四期已更加落實單面向等第檢核，並且更為重視所評等第之廣度，才能更加具有評分鑑別度，例如：請學系評分宜滿足「所有考生總分全距在20分以上」。其次，本校結合書審與面試評分系統，以建立完整的申請入學評分機制，使整套申請入學評分機制，皆可於系統上完成，因而更具便利性與時效性。再者，第四期已整合本校評分系統及未來學習歷程檔案評分系統，除了優化各項系統功能，也針對未來111學年度即將啟動全國學習歷程檔案的評分系統，與甄選會系統、暨南國際大學洪政欣教授團隊開發之系統交換經驗，期能整合出111學年度適合本校評分的系統。

三、未來可藉長期研究並納入就業表現，以明晰本校學生的學習與就業軌跡

本校已進行部分招生議題的校務研究分析，未來可發展更細緻內容，以輔助學校及學系進行招生策略的參考方針；後續可針對高中課程學習成果、多元表現，及大學的非學業表現多加探討，並且追蹤到畢業後就業，以進行高中、大學、就業之延續性調查，了解本校學生的學習與就業軌跡。在資料取得上與教育部密切合作，並且進行長年縱貫分析，以紮實地看出本校入學生的恆毅力、學習與就業軌跡，並提供更長遠的招生與校務發展策略。

本校基於以事證為本的校務決策精神，有效推動校內招生專業化的種種措施，包括：發展學系評量尺規、開發線上評分系統、執行多項招生議題分析等項。唯招生議題乃學校持續關注的核心項目，在今日少子化趨勢下更顯其重要性，本校須藉由招生專業化發展突顯本校招生優勢，以及招生專責辦公室中的分析規劃組、試務行政組、高中合作組等各組通力合作，協調其他單位的資源與需求，協助學系擇才。另一方面，在高中素養導向育才，以及大學專業化擇才之雙管齊下等作為，期許為新一代學子開啟更為多元與開放的學習風潮，也為台灣整體教育構築嶄新的希望、美好的願景與務實可行的做法。

參考文獻

沈碩彬（2020a年12月）。大學個人申請入學之招生決策有效性初探：以一所私校為例。**「2020 教師專業發展學術研討會」發表之論文**，國立中興大學。

沈碩彬（2020b）。高中、大學、就業之三位一體校務研究融合作法。**臺灣校務研究專業協會通訊，15**，6。

沈碩彬（2020c）。大學生入學前後表現關聯性初探：以一所私立大學為例。載於王俊權、林家禎、鄭志文（主編），之**「2020創新教學的自我對話：校務研究與大學社會責任研討會」論文集**（頁17-32）。靜宜大學。

沈碩彬、林家禎、鄭志文（2019）。招生專業化計畫結合校務研究之作法。載於鄭志文（主編），**2019多元升等暨教學實踐研究研討會論文集**（頁4-11）。靜宜大學多元升等制度專案辦公室。

沈碩彬、鄭志文（2019）。**從十二年國教之「學習歷程檔案」談高中與大學之課程合作**。「2019第十一屆教育專業發展學術研討會」發表之論文，東海大學。

沈碩彬、鄭志文、林家禎、葉介山（2019）。招生專業化發展試辦計畫的推行——以靜宜大學為例。**臺灣教育評論月刊，8**（11），87-92。
教育部高教司（2018）。**大學招生專業化發展試辦計畫**。教育部高教司。
教育部高教司（2020a）。**大學招生專業化發展計畫：109-110學年度計畫說明**。教育部高教司。
教育部高教司（2020b）。**大學招生專業化計畫——多元選才，讓每個人發光**。http://www.news.high.edu.tw/feature_story/content.php?cid=204&did=750
陳世宗（2020）。**靜宜大學「1=3」協助弱勢及準弱勢生翻轉未來**。中時晚報。https://www.chinatimes.com/realtimenews/20200701000805-260421?chdtv
楊川欽（2021，1月8日）。清水高中自主學習成果發表。**台灣新聞報**。https://www.twnewsdaily.com/home/news_pagein.php?iType=1002&n_id=91835
劉孟奇（2018）。**結合大學選才與高中育才**。http://www.kmsh.tn.edu.tw/km107/108-1080525-20min.pdf
賴信宏（2019）。**資料審查輔助系統與檢討機制**。招生專業化演講簡報內容，靜宜大學。
蘇偉順、沈碩彬、葉介山、林家禎、鄭志文（2020年10月）。大學個人申請網路書面審查系統之設計與建置。**「TANET2020台灣網際網路研討會」發表之論文**。台灣大學。
Cicchetti, D. V. (1994). Guidelines, criteria, and rules of thumb for evaluating normed and standardized assessment instruments in psychology. *Psychological Assessment, 6*(4), 284-290.

國家圖書館出版品預行編目

以資料為本的校務決策績效評估 / 臺灣校務研究專業協會著. 周景揚、王菈君主編 -- 新竹市 : 臺灣校務研究專業協會, 2022.11
面； 公分
ISBN 978-626-96614-0-4(平裝)

1.CST: 高等教育 2.CST: 學校行政 3.CST: 文集

525.607 111015042

以資料為本的校務決策績效評估

主　　編／周景揚、王菈君
出　　版／臺灣校務研究專業協會
地址：新竹市大學路1001號工程五館542室
電話：(03)5712121#50188
製作銷售／秀威資訊科技股份有限公司
114 台北市內湖區瑞光路76巷69號2樓
電話：+886-2-2796-3638
傳真：+886-2-2796-1377
網路訂購／秀威書店：https://store.showwe.tw
博客來網路書店：https://www.books.com.tw
三民網路書店：https://www.m.sanmin.com.tw
讀冊生活：https://www.taaze.tw

出版日期／2022年11月　　**定價**／320元

版權所有・翻印必究　All Rights Reserved
Printed in Taiwan